Madam Mayor

How I Learned to Love Government
And Hate Politics
In Ten Intriguing Years

Madam Mayor

How I Learned to Love Government
And Hate Politics
In Ten Intriguing Years

by
Marcy Meffert
Former Mayor, City of Leon Valley, Texas

To Carol

Enjoy

THE
WATERCRESS
PRESS
2006

Marcy Meffert

A Watercress Press book
from *Geron & Associates*
www.watercresspress.com

Book design by Fishead Design Studio & Microgallery

Photo on front cover by Gary M. Perkins.

To order additional copies of this book:
Marcy Meffert
P.O. Box 680262, Leon Valley TX 78268

Library of Congress Control Number 2006932654
ISBN-13: 978-0-934955-68-3
ISBN-10: 0-934955-68-9

DEDICATION

This book is especially dedicated to all who have asked me:
Why Would Anyone Want to Run for Public Office?
and
To all who are thinking of running for public office,
To those who are or have been elected officials,
To the voters who put them in office,
To the people who support them—family, friends, and colleagues
And finally, to those who taught me to love government
and hate politics.

Special thanks for serving as my "first reader" on this book to my
friend, neighbor, and colleague, former Leon Valley councilmember
Marilyn Bellows, who has taught American Culture at the University
of Texas at San Antonio and who is so very qualified to give editorial
advice on this subject.

CONTENTS

PREFACE

When the late President Harry Truman said, "If you can't stand the heat, stay out of the kitchen," he could have been talking about Bexar County suburban elections where the heat is both literal and figurative.

South Texas in late April is bound to be hot; it's nature's test of your will. I learned this while campaigning for council, and later for mayor, in Leon Valley, Texas, a suburb of about 10,000 population completely surrounded by the City of San Antonio.

Dancing what I call the Election Two-Step is mandatory and involves walking door-to-door until our Texas sun sears your skin, the temperatures bake your body, and you beg for relief from being fried on cement sidewalks and steamy asphalt driveways.

No doubt about it, Texas weather makes the kitchen literally hot. The heat is figurative when elections are vigorously contested and the heat comes from foes and friends, if indeed you can determine who are friends and who are foes, which is another test of your will. Paranoia reigns as campaigners and their enthusiastic and well-meaning representatives may "creatively" interpret campaign rhetoric and literature — if literature is the right term.

If you are a candidate like I was, who says she wants to run a positive campaign and explains that she is running *for* an office, not *against* a person, people with good intentions will attempt to "help" you by sharing the newest rumor about your opponent even if you've said you don't want to hear it.

The figurative heat can drain so much energy away from your ability to deal with the literal heat that you begin to understand what poet Maya Angelou meant when she warned us to avoid "being pecked to death by ducks." Sometimes the rumors that circulate about candidates are silly enough to may you cry fowl and substitute geese for Angelou's ducks.

Sometimes you *can* identify a potential foe. For example, I had a friendly, no-money bet with an experienced politico that I could run my campaign for $800. When I told only one person that buying yard signs would put me over budget (meaning the $800 of the bet), without explaining about the bet to that person, a rumor got started that I couldn't afford to run for office and that my campaign was funded by another candidate. Having funding from another candidate violated the custom in our city of running alone as opposed to running with a political clique.

"Running alone" becomes almost impossible because alliances form when candidates are supported (or not) by recent or past previous officeholders who no longer want to do the Election Two-Step but still like to go to the dance — like one's elderly aunts, uncles, and grandparents at a wedding.

I think that if you are the candidate, you appreciate having your political aunts, uncles, and grandparents clap and cheer when you dance, but you have to make it clear that you want to lead, not do a Ginger Rogers/Fred Astaire routine — as former Texas Governor Ann Richards noted — in which Ginger did everything Fred did but "danced backwards in high heels."

Sometimes you can tell who your friends are. They are the ones who offer to help you by walking door-to-door or making phone calls to deliver your message and literature. (Of course, yours is *literature*, your opponent's is not.) Having loyal friends keeps you cool, no matter what sort of heat is making you sweat. I was most fortunate to have a previous mayor, whom I dubbed Mayor Emeritus, as a friend, consultant, and political advisor. His name, Ken Alley, is synonymous with "good citizen" in our town.

There's an old Irish blessing that could be called "A Politician's Prayer." It deals with friends and foes and goes like this:

> May those who love us, love us.
> And those that don't love us,
> May God turn their hearts.
> And, if God does not turn their hearts,
> May he turn their ankles,
> So that we will know them by their limping.

The campaign challenges prepare you for the real challenge of holding office, which is the ultimate volunteer job in Texas where most city councilmembers and mayors either receive no salary at all or a very insignificant stipend for attending meetings. Lack of real salary is one reason so many non-officeholders ask us why we run for public office. I don't think that the word "reason" enters into any answer to the question, "Why would you want to hold a political office?"

Why would reasonable, rational people willingly, and sometimes at great sacrifice of time, energy, and money, expose themselves to judgment and criticism by other people who may or may not be always reasonable and rational?

My answer is: One always hopes that altruistic motives lead some people into leadership. Hope is what makes life worth living, despite certain realities. The reality of politics is that while some folks are genuinely altruistic, a whole lot of others run for political office because being in the spotlight, even if it's not mega-wattage, is a real ego trip. Also, one can actually enjoy the challenge of a campaign, at least the first time.

Once you are elected, especially to a local level political office, you learn that hills can be more challenging than mountains — especially when water running down those hills tends to flood a citizen's front yard instead of going down the sewer line.

Being in the spotlight at the local level means that people recognize you at the supermarket or, worse yet, at the pharmacy where you are picking up your Vagisil, Proscar, Viagra, or Cialis, and then ask you why the garbage truck went by and didn't pick up their tree limbs. People will call you to complain about bouncy potholes in their streets instead of calling city hall, because you said you'd "serve" and so you'd better get them some service.

The reality is that local politics has a lot to do with drainage, potholes, garbage, and sewers because your decisions affect people where they live. A local officeholder can't stop wars, solve international economic problems or eliminate world hunger and diseases, but local decisions directly affect the quality of the daily lives of people.

We can choose not to read about the current wars and world terrorism, but when sewers malfunction and our garbage is not collected, we can't choose to ignore the smell. When we have to waste a half-day getting a tire repaired because the street in front of our house has a pothole, we don't think about land mines, homemade explosives, or bomb craters in foreign countries.

Yet, although local politics affects our lives so directly, voting in local elections is even less important to many people than voting at higher levels of government. In some areas of Bexar County, there are people who don't even know that they live in a suburb of San Antonio instead of San Antonio itself, and there are some who don't know or care when or where local elections are held.

Despite all of the above, holding office in a small community (or in any other governmental entity) is an opportunity to accomplish good at a level that directly affects people's quality of life, whether or not they know you are doing good. It's as if you are being judged at Christmas time by Santa, and your reward is not a toy but the actual process of being "good for goodness' sake."

I believe that doing "good for goodness' sake," is the only reasonable and rational reason to run for a political office because such use of power is the ultimate and most rewarding ego trip of all.

Once you get elected, the lessons about the realities of political power come every day, at every meeting, with every encounter with citizens, business people, your fellow officials, and with those always daunting decisions about everything and anything and mostly things you never knew anything about.

For example, you may have run for office because you believed that when citizens protest, officials should vote as the citizens demand. After all, isn't that what good representation is? Didn't they vote for you so that you could vote for them?

Previous officeholders warned you that you many have to make unpopular decisions and take heat from voters, but you believed them the way you believed your mommy when she said, "Don't touch the stove; it's hot."

Most of us still have those defiant-toddler, terrible-twos scars on the tips of our fingers, but we don't relate them to our adult lives.

In the hot spotlights and cold light of the fluorescents above your city council's dais, you learn that you have to base decisions on their effects for the next 10, 15, or 20 years, not the next 10, 15, or 20 minutes while citizens are taking turns at the podium venting their ire. If it's a zoning issue, you have to consider that the owner of the property in question has rights, too, not just the owners of the surrounding properties.

Much has been written by great philosophers on "rights," but the citizen at the podium protesting commercial development near residential areas or a change in zoning doesn't care what Thomas Jefferson, John Locke, John Stuart Mill, and others have said about rights. That person cares about too many people in the neighborhood, increased traffic, too-bright lights at night, and aesthetics of fences facing the residential side of the neighborhood.

And who's to say the protestors aren't right about who has more rights? Scary as it seems, you are the one with the say about whose rights prevail!

Often, you vote for the lesser of two evils, and then nobody is happy, not even you. Sometimes you don't agree with your fellow officials and you must decide if you will vote against their concepts or projects and accept that some will then vote against your concepts and projects in retaliation. Sometimes your vote will prevent you from ever getting reelected to any office ever again — or so the citizen protesting at the podium is telling you.

You learn that consensus building is not just a term used in leadership workshops: It's a valuable tool for constructive action. Your first attempt at consensus building will have you trying to remember who first told you that life was a trade-off. And you may remember when you thought "trade-off" was a synonym for "sell-out."

I have always been the type of person who believed the old Texas saying, "The only things in the middle of the road are yellow lines and dead armadillos," and I was shocked at how often a moderate view is valid and how often I chose a moderate point of view. I learned that often when two extreme solutions bounce up and down like a teeter-totter at the park, only someone standing precariously in the middle can create enough balance to slow down the action so that all can get off with at least some dignity.

But then, dignity is not always the definitive word in politics where pratfall possibilities abound and many situations make you sweat.

While Harry Truman's admonition about staying out of the kitchen if you can't stand the heat is certainly valid, once you get into the political kitchen and start stirring up cauldrons of controversy, or if you find yourself in a stew, you may conclude that it's not just the heat; it's not just the humidity (drainage, sewers, street puddles in potholes); it's all that steam and hot air. And some of that hot air may be coming from you!

However, when all is said and done, if you have a good idea, and you can convince enough people to help you make it a reality, and if the result is a benefit to a whole lot of other people, you will have the highest possible high. And then you will know why you ran for public office and want to run for reelection to do it all over again.

GLOSSARY

The clues to all those acronyms that clutter up the text.

AACOG   Alamo Area Council of Governments

CAVE   Citizens Against Virtually Everything

EDT   Economic Development Tax

EPA   Environmental Protection Agency

FEMA   Federal Emergency Management Administration

GBCCC   Greater Bexar County Council of Cities

GOBS   Good Old Boys Society

SCAC   Small Cities Advisory Council

TML   Texas Municipal League

Madam Mayor

Chapter 1:

The Swearing In that Comes Before the Swearing At

"I (Your Name), do solemnly swear (or affirm), that I will faithfully execute the duties of the office of (Mayor, Councilmember, Commissioner) of the City of (Your City) of the State of Texas, and will to the best of my ability preserve, protect, and defend the Constitution and laws of the United States and of this State; and I furthermore solemnly swear (or affirm), that I have not directly nor indirectly paid, offered, or promised to pay, contributed, nor promised to contribute any money, or valuable thing, or promised any public office or employment, as a reward for the giving or withholding a vote at the election at which I was elected. So help me God."

With voice trembling, you recite the oath of office, lower your right hand, and then walk to the dais. You sit down in your very own place which is designated by a nameplate that has your name on it. And your name is preceded by a title! You are an elected official — a councilmember, mayor, trustee, judge, commissioner, senator, representative! No more just plain "Ms." or "Mr."

You look at the people in the audience, some of whom have voted for you and who are smiling and applauding. Others, who have not supported you, are scowling; their arms are folded across their chests in the "I don't want to hear what you have to say" position.

You look from side to side at the other people on the dias who will be your colleagues for the next couple of years. Some of them supported you, some may have worked for your opponent. They also may be smiling or scowling, or, in the interest of statesmanship, just placing their faces in neutral.

The gavel clacks the meeting to order. And it should be noted that the sound of the gavel is even more startling if you are the one holding it!

You begin to sweat under the hot spotlights. The awesome sense of "why did I do this and what did I get myself into" sinks into the pit of your churning stomach.

"Oh, yes," your brain kicks in, "I got elected because people liked my ideas and now I have a chance to implement those ideas. How good can life get?"

And that's when you feel like a mosquito in a nudist colony — you don't know where to begin.

✠ ✠ ✠ ✠ ✠

If you are newly elected, take comfort in the reality that you are not the only one who has had a moment of trepidation that first time you sat down to solve problems that you may or may not really understand, no matter how many times you read the material that staff presents to you before each meeting.

I was one of many newly elected councilmembers who took a deep breath and thought, "What have I got myself into?" To find out what other elected officials thought at that magic moment and during their tenures in office and to get material for this book, I passed out 99 survey forms to public officials I met through my various Texas Municipal League, Alamo Area Council of Governments, and Greater Bexar County Council of Cities committees. In scientific circles, one would say the survey was "randomized," because if I had the survey forms in my purse I simply handed them to anyone with whom I happened to be chatting at state, regional, and local events and asked the councilmembers, mayors, judges, school board trustees, or other elected official to please read the letter describing my plans for this book, to answer the questions, and then return the stamped self-addressed envelope to me. I received 29 responses, which marketing folks tell me is a most phenomenal response.

Here is the letter I gave to public officials to get their experiences:

"SO YOU WANT TO KNOW WHY ANYONE WOULD WANT TO HOLD ELECTIVE OFFICE IN A SMALL TOWN!
People who do not hold political office often wonder why reasonable, rational people would willingly, and sometimes at great sacrifice of time, energy, and money expose themselves to judgment and criticism by other people who may or may not be always reasonable and rational.

My experience has taught me that when all is said and done, holding office and volunteering in a small city is an opportunity to accomplish good at a level that directly affects people's quality of life — whether or not they know you are doing so. It's as if you are being judged at Christmas time by Santa, and your reward is not a toy but the actual process of "being good for goodness' sake." So, doing "good for goodness' sake" is the only reasonable and rational reason to run for political offices.

To better explain why people get into politics and what it's like to be an elected official, especially in a small city, I am planning to write a book about my experiences and those of others. There are so many misconceptions about why and how people run for office and what life in office is really like that I think a book with candid information would be of interest to elective officeholders and want-to-be-elected people.

I would like to include opinions and experiences from other officials and so I'm asking you to fill out this questionnaire form. Because I need to get real information if the book is to have any value, all of the information you give me will be totally confidential and only I will see it. None of it will be attributed to any person or city. Rather it will be paraphrased and used in general statements such as: "Most people who run for mayor have previously served on a city council or have been on a city board, commission, or committee." "City council campaigns in small cities require walking door to door." And so forth. Your answers need not even be in full sentences — phrases will do. I know that you are busy. If you need more space use another sheet of paper but please identify the answer with the question's number. I will ask you for a quote as the last question on the attached form. Having been misquoted so many times myself, and having been a reporter when "off the record" was still observed, you can be sure that your quote will be used exactly as you wrote it, attributed to you, with your name, city, and council position.

If you do not wish to be quoted, that's OK too, but do indicate that you do not wish to have your name used at all on the last question. Then I will blend whatever you write into general statements. If you have any questions, please call, fax, or email me at my home. Thank you for your help.

✛   ✛   ✛   ✛   ✛

What a comfort it was for me to read the responses and learn that I was not the only person who sat at the dais the first time with a churning jumble of feelings that included awe, trepidation, excitement, and the overwhelming realization that I was no longer an ordinary citizen but someone who had acquired the humbling and challenging responsibility for the "health, safety and welfare" of everyone in our city.

Some of the self-talk that went on in my mind and in the minds of those that responded to my survey included mixed emotions about how well prepared one can be to make the right decisions for the city and how much work would be involved in learning how to do the job. Some people felt honored, proud, and thrilled; others felt intimidated and afraid that they would say "something dumb." One respondent humorously wrote that the first thought upon being seated on the dais was, "I want my mommy!"

Several officials expressed a feeling of "disbelief" that they had actually won the election and had been sworn into office. Some had aspired to hold public office from childhood because they had family or other role models on their city's councils and were thrilled to be in their role models' council seats. One respondent, whose father had been a mayor, wrote, "I wished that my dad were alive to see me."

Some, who were among the first people of color in their communities to get elected, felt an acute awareness of making history and one wrote that thoughts of "A lot of people died for this opportunity" were awesome and humbling. Being elected mayor, after having served as a councilmember, brings a whole new set of feelings that include wondering how you will deal with the people with whom you have served for several years and whose idiosyncrasies have either annoyed, delighted, or just plain driven you crazy.

Chapter 2:

So Why Would Anyone Run for Political Office?

If it is so unsettling and scary, why do some people run for elective office? It surely isn't for money. While some cities pay elected officials, most Texas officeholders do not receive any salary or receive only a small salary that doesn't compare to what one would receive for a non-government job with similar responsibilities.

Believe it or not, my survey and my conversations with fellow public officials renewed my optimism about public service in that most ran for election because they "felt a duty to give back to the community" or "to improve the world into which I was born." They have a long history of community service and believe in volunteerism and want to contribute their talents, experience, and skills to benefit others, to improve the quality of life, and shape the future of their communities. Some people have always aspired to hold public office and/or got inspired by a cause or specific issue. Some simply found that they had the time and wanted to do something useful with it. Often, holding public office is attractive to retired people who have always had a desire for public service but not enough time while they were working at demanding jobs and fulfilling family obligations.

People who have been active in their communities in various appointed committees, commissions, and boards want to take the next step in the level of their involvement and that step is to run for elective office. Some feel that they can accomplish more being "on the inside" instead of being "on the outside" of the decision-making process, especially about certain issues. It's not unusual for a minister to run for office because holding public office is seen as an extension of ministry and the obligation to represent those in their congregations who may have been outsiders due to ethnicity, politics, or for other reasons.

Often, people are asked by their friends to run for office; others are recruited or pressured to run by various citizens and citizen groups. Some people run for office to provide generational balance to their council, court, or board of trustees. Others see an opportunity to work with certain progressive leaders in their communities. There may have been problems with the current councils or boards regarding decisions, decorum, and lack of leadership, especially that of an incumbent mayor. The mayor is an easy target. It doesn't matter if a council simply won't work together or, worse yet, some councilmembers gang up against the mayor. I learned early on that the person with the higher chair-back and who sits in the center of the dais is also at the center of any controversy.

In many cities, especially in small towns it seems, there may be a feeling that not all of the people have an equal voice in local government because their city has an organized political monopoly — a Good

Old Boys Society (GOBS in this book!). Some people run for office to run against the GOBS. GOBS can become so powerful in some cities that they have a core of people who wait to be told which candidate or which issue should get their votes.

The first time that I encountered somebody who said, "I vote like (GOB Power Broker) tells me to," I was shocked. As the years in office passed, my shock dissolved into dismay, and finally into despair. At first I wondered why good, intelligent people would vote blindly at the direction of someone else. And even after I was in office for a couple of years, I kept trying to understand why somebody would want to have that much control over so many people.

Finally, I concluded that for some people, power is an aphrodisiac, especially if and when they see the other phases of their lives going into decline. There may be other reasons to need such power, but I don't know what they are — yet. I don't think that all GOBS are bad for a community. Sometimes voter apathy is such that the GOBS, however ego-driven, are the only ones who care enough to take on the responsibility for running things. Some folks use their power to do good things, some use it to promote personal causes which may or may not benefit the community as a whole, and others just revel in the manipulations of the public either as elected insiders or as kingmakers who get others elected. I have also observed that some people, GOBS or non-GOBS, are bullies; probably were bullies when they were young and got worse as they aged and got into positions of power. Worse yet, once in power they can't seem to let go of it. Term limits can push GOBS and bullies out of office but then they also push non-GOBS out of office and here lies another of the dilemmas in government.

Here's a poem inspired (aggravated?) by political bullies, which I wrote after a particularly unpleasant meeting in which bullies actually bullied each other. (I don't know what non-writers do to vent their frustrations. I have the stress-relieving outlet of writing poetry, essays, and letters to the editors of various newspapers.)

THE POLITCAL BULLY
He stands
Not so small of stature but
Small of mind
Big of mouth
You get nothing but bull from a Bully.

He sits
Arms folded
To keep out
Any idea that's not his
Small mind, big mouth,
No space for new thoughts.

He talks
A diatribe inflicted upon us.
I'm just gruff, he says.
Oh yeah? The word is rude.
Small mind, big mouth
No reasonable reply accepted.

He sees
With blinders on
Tunnel vision prevails
Which makes him narrow minded
Small mind, big mouth
No progressive viewpoints noted.

He hears
Only his own words
His lips a megaphone
Assaulting the ears of others
Small mind, big mouth
Blustering bilious blather.

He inspires
Like-minded folks
Who fear the future
Who feel impending impotence
Who live in the good old days
Though the days are more old than good.

He stands
Not so small of stature but
Small of mind
Big of mouth
You get nothing but bull from a Bully.

by Marcy Meffert

While GOBS usually run for reelection because they can't let go
of power, many other dedicated officeholders run for reelection to
complete certain special projects that began during their administra-
tions. Some feel as if they are making progress and "making a difference" in the community, and so running for reelection is the best way
to continue community service. Many feel that they want to use the
knowledge and experience they gained during their first terms to do
even more good for their cities, school boards, and other entities. It's

a matter of "now that I know what I'm doing, I can do it better, and so I must run."

Others represented their city, school board, or other entity in regional, state, or national organizations and ran so that they could complete their tenures and fulfill their obligations to those groups. Some just liked the job and wanted to continue. One of my great regrets in choosing not to seek a fourth term as mayor of my city was that I was in line for leadership in TML's Association of Mayors, City Councilmembers, and Commissioners and had begun to serve on the board of the Texas Municipal League. Both positions were a unique and exciting challenge that would enable me to be a voice for my city and my region during the upcoming Texas Legislature sessions. Of course, other equally qualified people took my place who would certainly do a good job and that's a lesson a lot of people never learn — that we are all replaceable. I believe that thinking you are irreplaceable is an ego trip that can take you on the road to GOBS City.

GOBS City is inhabited by folks who think only they know everything, that only they are right all of the time, and that getting another point of view is a waste of their time. In GOBS City new ideas are suspect, and, in fact, often feared because new ideas spawn the dreaded C-Word — CHANGE. The words different and change are synonyms for wrong in GOBS City. However, a loss to the GOBS should not discourage a person, because some candidates who responded to my survey noted that they eventually did get elected despite the GOBS and despite those who wanted to maintain the status quo.

Many people run for office because they see things that they believe need changing and they also believe they are the ones who should cause that change. This attitude is not always good if the official is a one-issue candidate and after election all efforts are focused on that one issue to the neglect of everything else. However, if the official is open-minded — even about the main campaign issue — and also is concerned about the other needs of the city and the opinions and feelings of all the citizens, I don't think that being elected on one issue need be detrimental to the city. Being open-minded is vital, especially if you are elected to the office of mayor. There is a saying: "Minds are like parachutes; they function only when open." It's a valid saying, especially when that word *change* is uttered.

Chapter 3:

Why I Ran for City Council and Mayor

My road to public office zigged and zagged for nearly forty years as a homemaker, wife, and mother of five children, who did volunteer work with church and civic organizations — mostly as a diversion from housework and an opportunity to hang out with people who can feed themselves and cut their own meat at dinner. Then in the year of my sixtieth birthday I ran for election to city council in Leon Valley, Texas, because, to me, holding political office is the ultimate volunteer job.

Like my other volunteer jobs, I more or less happened upon an opportunity and took it because the idea intrigued me. In my second career — as a writer — I had been a reporter for weekly and daily newspapers, covering various city councils and school boards. When I sat through city council meetings, I always found myself thinking, "I could do that." Then one day I happened to meet a councilmember I knew from Leon Valley while we both were voting and, with his encouragement, began the process of fulfilling a childhood "impossible dream."

When I was a little girl, about six years old, the alderman from our precinct in Milwaukee, Wisconsin, where I grew up, lived across the street from my apartment house. I was in awe of him and wished that girls could be aldermen. And so in 1994, when women could and did aspire to public office, I took the opportunity to fire up my idealism and run for city council.

My idealism came from a movement that you don't hear much about anymore — the Christopher Movement, popular in the 1940s and 1950s. When I was in my teens, I read the Christopher Movement book *You Can Change the World* and was inspired. I knew that I could change the world as soon as I made it through my teens . . . when my skin cleared up . . . and when I became a mature, adult woman in my twenties. I had a lot of ideas just waiting to happen!

Unfortunately, my skin broke out again in my twenties and I still hadn't changed the world except to have added three more humans to it. But I knew that I would change the world in my thirties . . . when the children were older and didn't need me so much. Peter, Paul, and Mary were singing about each of us lighting "one little candle" — and I had a big box of farmer matches. I started being chairman of this or that project with church women's groups and learned how to chair a meeting and chair an event without alienating too many members of my group.

In my thirties I added two more humans to the world, became more active in the community, and I learned that to change the world you have to attend lots of committee meetings, which are chaired by people who also want to change the world, but only on their terms, using only their ideas. But, undaunted, I knew that when I was in my forties, and the children didn't need so much attention, and when I had more experience dealing with committees, I could change the world. That is if I ever stopped changing diapers.

In my forties, I found that committee meetings gave me headaches and, although our children didn't need so much attention, I wanted to focus on some of my own needs — to change attitudes, attain personal goals, follow my secret dreams. I still wanted to contribute my ideas and experience to my community, but changing the whole world was beginning to seem like a lot of trouble, possibly more than I wanted to tangle with, especially if it involved going to meetings. PTA, band booster, and church committee workers know what I'm talking about.

But I was still committed to changing a small corner of the world, and planned to do it when I achieved my personal goals and dreams, probably when I was in my fifties. During this time, I served as president or chairman of several organizations and learned how to work with a board of directors and I learned the most important leadership factor: The buck stops at the top. If anyone who has a job within the organization doesn't do the job, the person at the top steps in to get things done even at the last moment. If a job gets done but is not done well, it's considered the fault of the person at the top. There is no point in making excuses. The only thing to do is move on.

In the meantime, as I was learning how to lead others I had to deal with being forty. If you are forty plus, and especially if you are a stay-at-home woman (called a housewife in my day) you'll relate to my situation.

It was three months before my fortieth birthday when I had the great revelation that led to a total change in my life. It altered my family's lives as a secondary effect, since everyone had to become more self-sufficient because mom stopped being totally available to everyone as she had been for the past twenty years. Even my husband learned a few new tricks and that helped when I became mayor of our city and had endless meetings that interfered with my cooking his meals as I had when I was a full-time homemaker.

I remember my life-changing day clearly. There I was, staring into what the TV commercials of that time called the bathroom bowl, swishing blue foam around for what had to be the umpty-millionth time. My life began flashing before my eyes — or more accurately, flushing before my eyes — and my eyes wandered to my sneakers. With two daughters whose shoe sizes leaped ahead of mine, I had a lifetime supply of hand-me-down gym shoes with "Meffert" indelibly inscribed on their insteps. Being short, with a sprouting tall son, I had an equally abundant supply of inseam "short" jeans and my frugal upbringing required me to wear them out.

I looked at my reflection in the bathroom mirror, which I had just polished and which I knew would be steamed and smeared in a few hours when the grand teenage shower spree got going. The only garment I was wearing that was originally mine was my sweatshirt, and emblazoned across its front was, "They're coming to take me away. Ho ho, ha ha, hee hee." It was a gift from my husband, Rollie, when our fifth child was born — just one year to the day after our fourth child was born.

"Who are you anyway?" I asked that woman in the mirror. We were a military family, and I was a "dependent" so I knew my husband's social security number better than my own. Only his number would help me cash a check in the BX or get medical care at the base hospital for me and my also dependent children. When I went to my children's schools, I was somebody's anonymous mother. When I called the vet, I was the lady with four cats and the little brown dog with a bald spot on his rump, the result of his tangling with a weimaraner. Looking in the mirror I didn't feel like laughing " Ho ho, ha ha, hee hee!"

So I sent the blue foam swirling out of sight and I told myself that a woman who can learn to use bowl cleaner without reading the directions each time it's poured, swished, and flushed must have some reasonable level of intelligence. And if a husband could retire from the military after twenty years and have a second career, then why couldn't a wife retire from homemaking after twenty years and have a new career? In some newspapers they listed the occupations of people in their obituaries and one always saw Joe Bob Jones, 72, a retired engineer, or Billy Bob Lane, 83, a retired insurance salesman, but if Mrs. Effie Smith was a homemaker she was never a retired homemaker even if she was 95. Apparently one could not retire from homemaking which is just about the toughest job I ever had.

I retired from homemaking and bathroom cleaning that day and became a writer, my mid-step toward elective positions. Little did I know that my homemaking experiences would be a useful background for public office; clean water sources, properly flushing sewers, and drainage are important facets of city government. It should be noted that holding public office uses every type of personal and work experience you have had throughout your life. As a military officer's wife, I learned social skills that I hoped would be useful in some job and it definitely taught me how to work a crowd when I was campaigning and holding offices.

Changes had to happen in the Meffert household. In the midst of my middle-aged and identity crisis, I looked at the sneakers with

"Meffert" on the instep. "Marcy Meffert" will be a good byline and I will be a writer," I told the shoe, the hand-me-down jeans, the nearly prophetic sweatshirt, my reflection in the mirror, and the downstairs cat who was already slurping water from the newly sanitized bathroom bowl.

I marched directly to the phone and called the editor of a suburban weekly newspaper. I'd met the editor when delivering announcements of my Lackland AFB Officers' Wives' Club social functions — those functions where I had learned to work a crowd. I took a deep breath to stop my voice from quivering, told her that people always said I had a way with words and often asked "Can I use that line?" So now I wanted to use my own lines as a funny housewife columnist, I could be the Irma Bombeck of San Antonio, and I would work for nothing for three weeks. I should add here that a sense of humor and an ability to see the absurdities of life also are invaluable traits for holding public office if you are to retain your sanity when your idealism gets bashed and pummeled.

The column was a success and after a few weeks it got a name — "Cactus Garden." The name came from my belief that life is like a cactus garden — it's beautiful or ugly depending upon your attitude toward cactus . . . and whether or not you are being stuck by it at the moment. Humor is like rain on the ocotillo — a cactus that looks like a bunch of ugly brown, dried-up, thorny twigs until it rains, and then the ocotillo branches sprout tiny green leaves and delicate bright orange-red flowers that perch like butterflies on its thorny branches. Rain brings beauty to the desert like humor brings beauty to life. Since then, I have learned that political life also is like a cactus garden.

I went on from weekly papers to staff writing positions at a daily paper, then to producing talk radio shows, freelance writing in San Antonio and later in New Orleans. One of my jobs was editorial consultant to Heloise, the internationally syndicated lifestyle columnist, and so it seemed as if I'd gone full cycle from being in charge of my family's lifestyle to becoming a lifestyle consultant.

The communications business is fun and an excellent preparation for public life. You meet a lot of interesting people and each one gives you a lesson in how to communicate better. I wrote a personal column for more than five years, wrote editorials, and reported on city council and school board meetings, all of which taught me how to accept criticism from editors and readers. Developing a thick skin is definitely a preparation for holding public office. After I was elected I learned that it is much easier to write an editorial about what should or should not be done by a governing body than it is to actually get something done or prevent something from happening.

When I returned to college at age fifty, I developed a whole new appreciation for what my children were going through. But the greater benefit was the opportunity to associate with generations other than mine on a more equal footing and to learn from them. I found that with your own children you are a mom or dad, but with your fellow students you are a buddy even if you are too married to go bar-hopping with them on weekends. My classmates in a TV/radio class always urged me to adopt a "more womanly" lower-toned voice instead of my rather young-girlish voice. It made us all laugh since I was twenty years older than the professor and the students were younger than most of my children! The radio and TV classes were useful later in politics because they gave me poise when being interviewed about city issues. Lowering the tone of my voice also was a benefit because a well-modulated voice sounds more like you are the in-charge person when you are sitting on a dais or speaking to a group.

I returned to college again at fifty-five and again at age sixty — my plan was to get my bachelor's degree before I collected social security. But, like my plan to lose two pounds for each of the original thirteen colonies during the 1976 bicentennial year, my education plan took a detour and I got involved with other things. Still, many of the subjects I took were useful in my political career, such as several philosophy courses (politics, religion) and anthropology courses. In one anthropology course, I learned that in the language of primitive tribal societies usually the word that means "us" or "members of our tribe" is the word that compares to "human", and the word that refers to "them" or "members of other tribes" is a word that compares to "animal" or "less than/ not human." "Us" being "human" and "them" being "not human" seems to say it all about international politics for sure and sometimes about local politics.

By the end of my fifties, I actually had attained some of my goals: I was almost a junior in college, had fulfilled my secret dream of becoming a writer, and had adjusted my attitudes. I still thought the world needed some changing but it would involve getting a lot of people to change — and by the time you reach age fifty you learn that the only person you can change is yourself.

Also in my fifties I began to notice that of the people in this world who needed changing a small percentage of them aren't worth bothering with; many don't want to change and therefore won't under any circumstances. The remainder want changing but not by me. Another revelation that hit me around the end of this decade was that I'm probably not qualified to judge who and what in this world needs change — and that's a major attitude adjustment! And it's an adjustment most of us would like the rest of the world to make. It is also an adjustment that, in politics, enables you to deal with the CAVE (Citizens Against Virtually Everything) people.

My life changed again when I had sixty candles on my birthday cake. I looked at my reflection in the bathroom mirror — the same bathroom in which I made the decision to retire from homemaking twenty years before — and asked myself: Do I still want to light Peter, Paul, and Mary's little candle or do I want to sing a different tune? Is it time to leave the world-changing up to my children or the children of the people I've met in committee meetings.

Well, I concluded, *my* children? Sure! But other people's children? I wasn't so sure.

Then one day I realized that I didn't have to wait for my children to change the world. I could at least get the changing started. That's when I went to vote in a November election, and at the polling place I met Leon Valley Councilmember Ken Ward who served on the council while I was a reporter. He told me who was running for office that spring in Leon Valley. I told him that I always thought that I could do as well as the folks about whom I wrote. He said, "Why don't you run?" and I said, "I think I will." I went immediately to Leon Valley City Hall, picked up an election packet, and filed for city council and won.

So at age sixty I began the first of my two terms on the Leon Valley City Council and discovered that I still had that big box of matches and I still wanted to light a candle, even if it lit up only a small city in Texas. Then, after two two-year terms on council, I ran for mayor so that I could carry that candle around for a couple more years.

There was a poster on the wall in my office at city hall that I hoped would inspire visitors. It quotes the anthropologist Margaret Mead, who said :

Never Doubt That a Small Group of Thoughtful Committed Citizens Can Change the World: Indeed It's the Only Thing That Ever Has.

I ran, unopposed, for mayor for two more terms. When I chose not to run for office after six years on the job and ten years total on council, I presented a bronze plaque to the city engraved with the Mead quote with the hope that people would continue to read her truism. I also hoped that the city's numerous volunteer organizations would put up plaques with their service mottoes so that everyone who came to city hall would walk past a "Wall of Volunteering Honor" and be inspired. I'm not sure this will happen but I remain optimistic. (I should point out that a citizen who disagreed with one of my votes said at a council meeting that the plaque looked like graffiti, which shows how even your best intentions can be criticized and maligned.)

When you get involved in politics at the local level, you soon learn that the issues are not world peace, world hunger, or the global economy but drainage, potholes, garbage, sewers, and neighborhood code compliance . . . things that directly affect people where they live. Even when there is war in the Middle East, scandal in the White House, or an El Niño or La Niña is making crazy weather, people are most upset if the streets flood, sewers don't flow, the garbage is not picked up on time, if they ruin a tire on a chughole, or their neighbor doesn't mow his lawn often enough. And yes, one time or another you do get asked if you can fix traffic tickets and/or code violation citations.

One night, in my first week as mayor, my husband and I were awaked at 11:30 p.m. by a young male voice asking me what I was going to do about our rude police officers. The voice went on and on about how badly the young man had been treated. Finally I was able to calm him down enough to take his name and number. I promised to call in the morning. When I checked with the police the next day, I learned that this boy had "earned" several traffic tickets, and that he lived with his mom who was not happy with his driving, and that particular night he was tail-gating an ambulance on a call so that he could speed — or so he thought. The "rude" police officer stopped him and gave him a ticket and a lecture on how he was endangering not only himself but the patient in the ambulance and the emergency personnel, too. And the story gets better. Previously, the kid's mom had told our police that if her son got another ticket she would take away his car keys if the judge didn't take away his license.

The lesson learned here is that when you get a complaint about the police or any other city staffer, you first need to get the other side. In ten years of hearing complaints, I found that the problems were only rarely caused by city staff. Frequently city staff are the messengers who tell people about, and are tasked with, enforcement of laws and city codes that people don't like, and since they are on the first line of fire, the complaint is often launched at the staffer, but the citizen's anger is really about the codes or laws — or the council that passed them.

In 2004, I chose not to run for public office and to pursue personal goals, one of which was to write books — this book especially.

I had made changes in my small corner of the world, my suburban city; and deep in my heart of hearts, I believe that I can still, at the age of seventy-one as this book is being written, make some sort of contribution toward making some part of the world a better place. My candle has not burned out and I hope that I can light the way for other late bloomers like me. Perhaps this book will inspire others to run for elective office or at the very least, become a volunteer in government.

Age should not be a factor. "Old" is usually twenty years older than you are. Actually, I prefer the term "chronologically challenged." Also, some people are old geezers when they are twenty, thirty, or forty, and some people retain their fire no matter what their age or what roads they have traveled or been dragged over.

Surely no chronological age is the end of the road if you still have some place you want to go. After all, as this book is being written, Peter and Paul are bald, and Mary is fat, but they are still singing "Don't let the light go out" to a whole new generation who seem eager to listen.

Everything is always possible. I have a small poster that says, "We are most alive when we do something, go somewhere, accomplish something we thought impossible. At that moment, that exhilarating moment, there is only joy — blessed unadulterated joy!" (*The World of Richard Stine*)

That exhilaration gradually grows as you proceed through your first meeting, and can continue throughout your term of office if you allow your mind to remain open, your attitude to remain flexible, and your ego to be kept in restraints. Then, unlike a mosquito in a nudist colony who doesn't know where to begin, you will know where to begin and you will change your corner of the world for the better.

Chapter 4:

Campaigning

For some people, campaigns are fun and games. For others, campaigns are really an ordeal. It can be entertaining to go door-to-door and meet your fellow citizens, their children, and their pets as you must do when campaigning in a small town.

A teenager answered the door at one home, and before I finished saying, "Hello, I'm Marcy Meffert and I'm campaigning for city council," the teen launched into a tirade about all the traffic tickets she was unjustly receiving from our city's police officers. The dad, standing behind the irate teen, stepped forward and said, "You tell those cops to give all the tickets that they see fit. I want to see this child get to the age of twenty-one." As a mom of five, I surely empathized with the dad.

At one home, a cute little Yorkie piled stuffed animals at my feet as I talked to the homeowner about my ideas for the city. The people told me that I had their vote because the dog gave her stuffed animals only to folks she liked and apparently was a good judge of people.

At another home, an ankle-biter little dog clamped its teeth on my pant leg as I tried to walk away and it was like something out of a cartoon as I dragged my leg with dog attached down the sidewalk. Apparently, this dog didn't like me — or did like me as a potential snack!

At yet another home, as I got onto the porch two huge dogs — one a Doberman and the other a scary blur in my mental picture collection — lunged at a screen door which I discovered, much to my intense horror, was not locked and apparently had a defective latch. I held the door shut to save myself from becoming their chew toy. Finally the homeowner approached and controlled the dogs. We had a very brief conversation and I left my brochure on the porch before I fled, grateful that the resident was home to deal with the two beasties; otherwise I might have spent several more terrifying hours holding the door shut and wondering why I was running for office anyhow.

Now I could add here that my last year in office was equally scary as I tried to protect myself from rabid councilmembers, but biting words don't make you bleed like biting dogs do. Still, I could say it was great training for the job of mayor.

But not all encounters are scary. Often people would invite me in for an iced tea or coffee. During one campaign, the man who answered the door said, "Meffert? Do you know a Dr. Meffert?"

"Yes, that's my husband, but he's retired," I replied.

"Retired?" The man gave me a very strange look. "But I just saw him in Dermatology at Lackland last month."

"Oh, that's my son, Dr. *Jeff* Meffert. My husband is a dentist, Dr. *Roland* Meffert." I imagined that the man was wondering why an old lady like me was married to such a young man as my son. What made the encounter such fun was he had many words of praise for my son, and every mother thrives on that.

Campaigning in a small city that is completely surrounded by a big city like San Antonio has its own peculiarities. After speaking to a citizen who decided to vote for me, I was asked where voting was held.

"At city hall," I said.

"You mean I have to go all the way downtown to vote?" the citizen gasped.

"Downtown Leon Valley," I replied, giving directions to city hall.

Evidently this citizen, like many others, did not know that we were in Leon Valley and not San Antonio. City borders are not always noticed, even by people who have lived in the cities for years.

As a budding gardener, I would ask people about their plants when we chatted at their doors and often they gave me cuttings, many of which are still growing in my yard ten years later. Sharing plants is definitely a bonding experience.

While campaigning door-to-door, I had a habit of collecting names of people who might serve on committees. After a couple of campaigns, I learned that people often volunteer when they are enthused after talking to you, but when the time comes to actually work on a committee many won't show up. But as noted elsewhere in this book, people in politics are optimists and so I continued to collect names and did get some loyal volunteers on the campaign trails. That's part of the fun of meeting your fellow citizens and continuing the friendly relations with them after the election.

Campaigning for office takes more energy that anyone imagines — an under-statement if ever there was one. You meet more people than you have in your whole entire life, no matter what kind of life you have led. And while they are almost certain to remember you and your name, you need to have an extraordinary memory to remember all of their names. No matter how hard you try, it's a challenge to remember the names of the people whose hands you shook when you shook more than fifty or a hundred or more hands at a campaign event or to connect the names and faces of people you meet campaigning door-to-door, as you must in a small town, or a single member district of the school board of a larger city, and of course it's even more difficult for county, state, or national office.

You are more likely to remember faces but no names and, while you can use certain games such as associating names with certain characteristics, my experience is that you can't really fake it. It's better to confess that you can't remember the name than to commit a faux pas with some name game gone wrong. Like all things in public life, it's best to follow Rule Number 1: Always tell the truth. Then, you don't have to remember what you said.

Name Games

Many years ago, when I was in my thirties and still believed everything that was printed, I tried a name game that I'd read in a book which was obviously written by somebody who plays games better than I do.

The scene: I am presiding over a meeting and have just asked for volunteers, and a woman in the front row raises her hand to volunteer. She's been at many meetings and I should know her name but I cannot conjure it up from my brain cells which seem to have suddenly shut down. So, cleverly following the book's advice, I ask, "Now how do you spell your last name again?"

"J-O-N-E-S," she replies, eyes narrowed, to produce a look that could kill.

Needless to say, I never tried that trick again.

We had three women in our city who looked the same to me unless all three were present at the same event and my eyes could compare them to each other. I dealt with this problem by never using any of their names for fear I would use the wrong one. I don't recommend doing as I did but it worked for me. I would rather use no name than use the wrong one.

One of the judges who served on the Alamo Area Council of Governments (AACOG) had a great way of asking questions. He would say, "I guess I'm dumb on Tuesdays (or whatever day it was) but I don't understand what you just said." The "dumb on Tuesdays" approach can be used as a preface when you have to say, "I guess I'm dumb today but I'm sorry I forgot your name."

The usual excuse people use is that they just don't remember names and it seems acceptable, since a lot of people don't remember names. However, if you can learn to remember the names of people wherever you meet them, you will be way ahead of the game no matter what game you are playing! When meeting a lot of people, I try to remember at least one, or better three names of people I just met. Sometimes I succeed; sometimes I don't. Which brings me to Rule Number 2 of Public Life: If people see that you are sincerely trying to do the right thing, they will forgive your mistakes.

In our city, as in other cities, you get the legal rules for campaigning when you decide to run for office. It comes in a packet that you absolutely must read to find out who can file, how to file, when to file, where to file, and what information to report. *Why* anyone files is noted in Chapter 2 dealing with why people run for office.

✥   ✥   ✥   ✥   ✥

On my survey, I asked several questions about campaigning, and here are the questions and answers from the officeholders who responded.

What Is Your Best Practical Advice for Running a Campaign?

The most consistent advice from most of those who responded to my survey was to start getting organized early and to surround yourself with trustworthy supporters. Here are some do's and don'ts of campaigning from those who have walked door-to-door, attended umpteen events to meet and greet, and know what it's like to have tired achy feet and/or sore ears, neck and shoulder pain from calling citizens on the phone to "get out the vote on election day." I've also included some of my own comments and experiences here.

- Before you decide to run, make sure you really want to run for office and that you really enjoy meeting people and talking to groups. Recently, a newly elected mayor who had never held any office before, and apparently had no idea what being mayor entailed, expressed shock upon learning that "People call you all the time; the phone rings at all hours!" Experienced folks just laughed and said, "It comes with the territory; get used to it."
- Read and educate yourself; you need to be more informed than the average person. (Note that few things are as embarrassing as shooting off your mouth about something and finding out that whatever you were saying was so off-base and so ill-informed that you look as if you have no idea of what is going on and couldn't possibly be trusted to represent anyone in your constituency. Only the late comedienne Gilda Radner as Roseanne Roseannadana on the old "Saturday Night Live" show could get away with "Never mind.")

• Attend leadership programs, conferences, and workshops when they are available, and any other meetings or events where you can get informed. There are many opportunities after election to learn from seminars, workshops, and conventions with the Texas Municipal League (TML), regional meetings of the various districts of TML and workshops by COGS (Councils of Governments). Before election, you can get informed by reading local newspapers and attending meetings of the government in which you want to hold office. Our city had a Community Leadership Program for its citizens, and several other cities in Texas have similar programs. You can also learn by volunteering to work on various committees.

• Go to meetings of the council, board, etc., for several months before the campaign season starts so that you know what you are getting into, can get background information on issues, and can learn about procedures and policies.

• Love your government — city, county, school district, etc., and the people it serves. If you really care, it will show when you campaign and help you to win. Also, if you really care about what happens in your government, you can deal with any adversity that arises and enjoy all of the successes that are bound to occur during the campaign and while you hold office — if you win.

• Make sure you have a base of support, that you can offer an improvement over your opponent, and that you are in a position to campaign door-to-door and/or attend various events to meet and greet prospective voters. Serving on committees helps give you a base of support and helps people know your name from activities reported in newspapers. If your opponent is an incumbent, attending meetings and working with committees will get you some inside information about that opponent that will help you choose issues on which to focus in your campaign and also to do the job better if you win.

• Start getting organized early; you need to have a definite plan, plenty of supporters and money. The earlier the better, especially if, in addition to finding supporters with money for your campaign, you need to find people to help with mail-outs, walking door-to-door, and phone banks.

• Have a trustworthy core group of smart and energetic people to help with strategic planning and timelines. Timelines are really important so that you don't miss getting your materials mailed on time for early voting; timelines help you plan your events so that they are held at strategic times. Also, the timelines for reporting financial information are vital. If you don't properly report your finances, your opponent can claim that you should not be elected because you are a sloppy bookkeeper and so will not be a good steward with the voters' tax money. And who's to say that isn't true?

• Start early to raise money ethically and accept only money that doesn't hint at conflict of interest. Your common sense and ethical instincts will set off mental alarms if a donor seems to be trying to buy you. If you have any questions about such matters, consult with the election supervisor or an attorney who is knowledgeable about government. My rule is the one I learned as a writer while deciding what information should be in or cut out of any story: "If in doubt, leave it out."

In my first council campaign, a person who was a friend of a friend of another candidate (which should have set off a mental smoke alarm right there but I was very naïve at first) wanted to meet me for lunch. After lunch, I was taken to see a property that this person was considering purchasing as a possible site for a miniature golf course. My first comment to him was that it was adjacent to the backyards of a neighborhood and I thought people might not like having a harshly lighted, noisy business that stays open until midnight right behind their properties.

"Do you mean that you wouldn't vote for a zoning change on this property if you get elected?" the (until then) prospective campaign contributor asked.

"I mean that I don't want to talk to you anymore," I replied, vowing to always beware of friends of friends of anybody ever again, including friends of people I was certain were trying to help me. I was so very glad that I had driven to the site in my own car. It would have been awkward, to say the least, to drive back to my car with the now very irate "investor."

• Talk to people and as many groups as possible, especially those who will help you to "get the big picture." Campaigning helps you to learn that there are more issues than you may have realized and that after election you will have to prioritize issues and needs for the betterment of the whole city, school district, county, etc.

• If you have opposition for the office, you must make a major effort to reach as many people as possible. Elections where only plurality, not a majority, is required have been won by just a few votes or as has happened in small cities, by one vote. Every person you can convince is important!

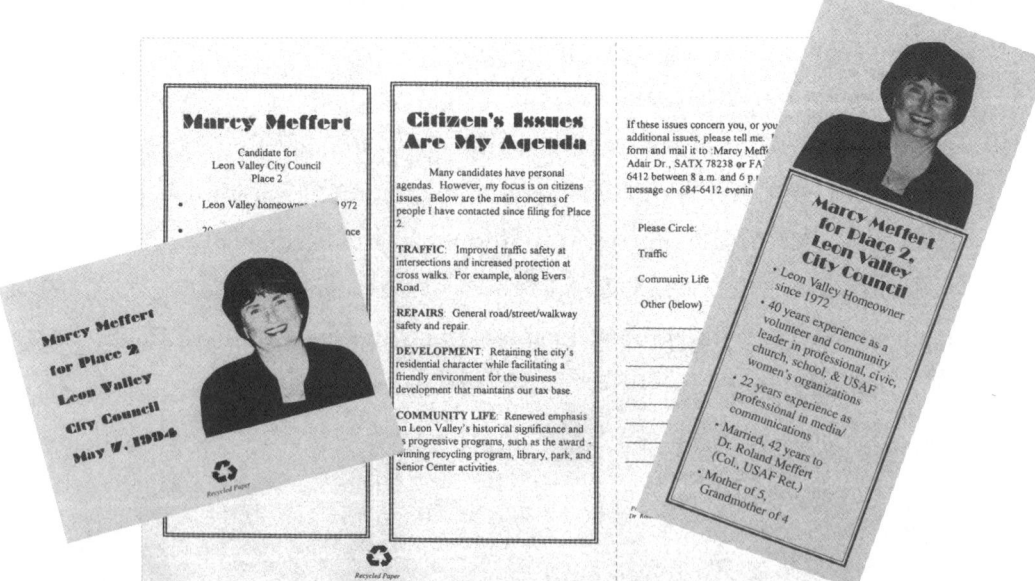

• Be prepared and be vigilant; know your opponents' strengths and weaknesses and then tailor your messages accordingly. Without slinging mud, you can present your message so that people can see that your ideas are better. For example, if your opponent has never held any office or served on any relevant committees, you can bring focus on your experience, chairmanships, successes, and what you have learned from your (gasp!) mistakes.

• Take the high road always. If you always tell the truth and take this advice, even if you lose, you will still have your loyal friends and supporters with you for the next campaign.

• Talk about only positive things and sell yourself instead of "blasting your opponents." Do think about the mud-slinging campaigns that you have seen in the past and try to remember what your attitude toward the "slingers" was when the campaigns got nasty.

• In your campaign literature and talks, confront all criticisms of your candidacy with positive answers. If you can say, "I understand what you are saying but consider this . . ." you will appear to be a reasonable person and, who knows, you may learn something that will make your campaign better and help you serve better after you win the election.

• Use words carefully and wisely in your speeches and advertising. It may be helpful to test your speeches with a knowledgeable, trustworthy person just as writers test works with an editor/first-reader. What's perfectly clear to you may not be perfectly, or even minimally, clear to someone else.

• Be honest and forthright in your campaign. The rule of "tell the truth so that you don't have to remember what you said" applies here.

• State your goals clearly and vote your promises after you win. But don't promise what you can't deliver and don't offer favors for votes. There is an old saying, "Under-promise and over-deliver," that carries a lot of truth. People will remember what you said. If you say in your campaigning, "This town needs more parkland," people will be expecting parks to be built after you are elected. If you say that taxes are too high and expenses must be cut, people will be expecting you to lower taxes and cut expenses even if, after you actually read a budget, you realize that the city needs more money, especially to build that park you promised.

• Connect with people and/or make sure they connect with you. Talk and engage with your citizens and remember the value of listening.

When campaigning and later while in office, I found it helpful to carry a small pocket-sized ring-bound notebook in which to write down names, phone numbers, and email addresses of people and the questions that they asked so that I could get the answers and call/email them back. The advantage is that you end up with a collection of people who have special interests and skills who can be appointed to various committees after you are elected. I would write names of people who asked questions and names of people who wanted to be on committees in the front of the book and flip the notebook to the back pages to make my "to-do" lists as I thought of "to-dos" while campaigning. As I did my "to-dos" I could rip off the page and feel as if something had been accomplished.

• Don't run for office with an axe to grind — that is to say, don't be a one-cause candidate. After you get elected you will be representing *all* of the citizens, young and old, pleasant and cantankerous, including those you don't know, don't like, don't agree with, and those who don't care to know you, don't like you, don't agree with you, and didn't vote for you and may have told you so in language that was abusive and rude.

• Invest in lots of all-weather yard signs and put them out early in the campaign. Name recognition is a worthy goal.

• When you campaign door-to-door, don't skip knocking on doors of people who display your opponents' yard signs. Some people will put up anybody's yard sign but it is not necessarily a signal that they will actually vote for that candidate, or that they will vote at all! We had a dear lady in our city who would put up anyone's signs and then her children would come and take them all down! She just couldn't or didn't want to say "No."

• Mail only to those who vote in municipal elections. In Bexar County, and I imagine elsewhere, there is an election service that provides mail-out, walk, and call lists with names of frequent voters. The lists include information on age, if the voter usually votes early (as many seniors do), and the elections in which the voter has voted in the last five years. There is a fee for this service but the fee is offset by your not mailing to non-voters.

You can also get a list from the city of those who voted in the previous election; you will be charged a fee for this but the names will be alphabetical which is useful for mailing but not for walking door-to-door. An election service provides the list of voters grouped by streets, which is what you need to determine who the voters are on each street. If you have software that can sort the names by street, you can scan or enter the names into your computer and make your own list, but it's really easier to have the service do it.

• Make sure you have comfortable shoes and plenty of time to meet and greet people. Note that when you are not walking you are standing to meet people, and comfortable shoes are a significant factor in enjoying/surviving a campaign!

• Develop a thick skin and learn to roll with the punches. Politics can be a contact sport — at least verbally! You mustn't take all the barbs personally even if they seem personal. You often meet people who are angry with the federal government but vent their ire on local candidates because we are the ones they can complain to or cuss at face-to-face! One survey respondent said, "When I run out of 'skin-thickening lotion' it is the worst part of campaigning and office holding." The respondent added the "skin-thickening lotion" compares to sunscreen and is vital because "caring so much can get you burned if you are not protected."

• Finally, have a cadre of at least six people "who love you no matter what" so that you have a soft place to fall when the going gets tough. One former councilmember told me that having friends who will let you spend a few rest and rehabilitation days of hiding out in their homes — away from your telephone — can really help you to reenergize your campaign if you feel like you are getting burned out.

What Did it Cost You in Money, Time, and Energy to Run?

Campaigns are really easy when you are the only candidate for the office you seek; you don't have to campaign at all and it doesn't cost a thing in money, time, or energy. However, not everyone is that lucky.

Campaign spending reported on my survey for smaller city campaigns and school boards ranged from no cost at all, to $100 of personal money, to several hundred thousand dollars in some bigger city campaigns. One campaign for mayor in a small city cost about $1,500 to $2,000, and reelection about $800 because yard signs from the previous campaign were still useable. My first campaign for council cost about $800 but my first campaign for mayor cost $1,200–$1,800 due to the purchase of signs and increased mail-outs.

Running for county office naturally costs more than for a small city office. One candidate said it cost about $8,000 and one year of time and energy for the first campaign; the second time it took $5,000 and a year but most expenses were borne by a local political organization and the most out-of-pocket was about $1,000. A state office candidate's campaign costs were just under $1 million.

When you are figuring out campaign costs, you need to consider that in Texas where most city officials serve without pay, holding office will cost you money in terms of some unreimbursed luncheons and personally funded gas for miles that you forget to record. You will also be expected to buy things that non-profits are selling, especially if the sellers are children, and people appreciate it if you contribute to gifts and memorials for birthdays, weddings, funerals. I finally decided that everyone who asked for a donation would get a $25 check and even then, at the end of the year I would be surprised at how much money I had dispensed. One year it was $2,000.

One respondent said that the cost in time is difficult to say because it's "a continual process." While several respondents said that although they enjoyed meeting their fellow citizens, walking door-to-door was physically exhausting. However, another said that campaigning "Energizes me!" One respondent said that the worst thing about running for election and holding office was running for reelection. In a reelection campaign, you can't claim that you will do a better job and provide more new benefits to the public than your opponent can. If you do, then someone is bound to ask why didn't you already do a better job since you had the opportunity during your previous term.

The most regretted cost of any campaign was time away from family and lack of time for personal life, including relaxation, recreation, and simple "thinking time" alone. Once you start a campaign, you are campaigning all of your time — at any public place and gathering including the supermarket, church (yes, regretfully at church!), and at home where the phone rings incessantly. One respondent felt that families were cheated when a candidate runs for office due to the time it takes to campaign and later to properly perform the duties of office.

Even when you are alone, your mind is campaigning as you try to remember if you have offended or neglected anyone at the last event you attended and what you will say to whom at the next event on your schedule. Perhaps there are some people who have an off switch and can put campaigning on the back burner when they need a break but I haven't met any of them yet.

What Was the Most Expensive Thing about Your Election Campaign?

Advertising in all forms was the most expensive thing in most of the campaigns of those who had expenses. For some it was the printing and mailing costs of campaign literature. (Note: Of course, *your* campaign materials are literature; your opponents' materials are junk mail and propaganda!) For one candidate, the most expensive things were signs, radio/print ads, and a post-election reception — which were all about equal in cost. Obviously, the office level you seek determines the cost of your campaign.

• Brochures/Pamphlets

If you think you will be running for office in the future, and running your own campaign, collect campaign literature from other people to get ideas about layout and content, colors and designs. You want to coordinate all the colors and typefaces of all printed materials so that when people see any of your materials they will associate the colors, typefaces, design/style with your name. Printers can be very helpful, especially if they have had experience printing campaign materials for other people; get referrals from other candidates. You will also want to choose colors that distinguish your materials from those of other candidates.

In all of my campaigns, I designed pamphlets that had a detachable postcard section which people could mail back to me with their ideas on what is important for our city. I had several people tell me that they voted for me because nobody had ever asked them to write their opinions before. I also had someone say that I must be getting money from somewhere to be able to have such a "fancy brochure." The fact is that, as a free-lance writer, I had written pamphlets and brochures for other people and businesses. Why shouldn't I write a nice one for myself?

In my first campaign, the brochure cost more because I had the printer perforate the line to tear off for the postcard. There was an extra fee for perforation and I had to buy heavier paper which cost more than suitable postcard stock. In subsequent campaigns, I had a dotted line printed with the traditional tiny scissors on the line to indicate that people could cut off the postcard for return mail. One side of the postcard asked for voter opinions about some key issues and had lines for their priorities; the other side was printed with my address, lines for the senders' return address, and that ubiquitous little box that says "Please place stamp here."

I had all my materials printed on recycled paper because I believe that we should all use it when possible; some people appreciated that and many didn't notice. I accepted that choosing more costly recycled paper for my printed materials was my first lesson in "doing good for goodness' sake" whether or not anyone cared or noticed. I cared. I noticed, and that was good enough for me.

I recall one candidate who gave out campaign handout cards, about 3x5, that were printed on one side with the city's office hours, library hours, and other information that people might want to save and a brief resume on the other side. I'll bet that fewer of these campaign materials were tossed out than is usually the case.

• Bulk Mail

I used a mailing service and if you also use one, know that you need to get the mailing service's bulk-mail permit number printed on your mail-out materials address section. In my first campaign, I investigated getting my own bulk-mail permit and doing my own mail-out and discovered that it actually saved postage to use a service which not only gets a better rate due to the service's volume but also can guarantee delivery on a target date. Smaller sacks of bulk mail can sit on a shelf to be mailed whenever but larger batches of bulk mail, such as that from a mailing service, generally get priority. The target date for most mail-outs is that the missive should be delivered on the day before or the very day early voting begins. The number of early voters increases every year to the point where sometimes half of the votes are early. And it's generally believed that senior citizens vote in great numbers and that senior voters frequently vote early, so you want to get your materials out on time.

• Yard Signs

Yard signs were my biggest expense. Leon Valley's population is 10,000 with about 5,000–6,000 registered voters and with about

1,200 to 1,800 on the frequent-voter list. I decided that 100 yard signs, strategically posted, would be all that I could place in my first mayoral campaign. (I didn't use signs in my council campaigns.) Then I found that more people wanted signs than I had bought so I had to have more printed. I could have saved some money by having more printed the first time around. I bought plastic signs which are placed into the ground with wire holders. Paper signs are cheaper, but they have to be nailed to wooden picket-fence type holders. Our city has many yards which have only a little topsoil over hard caliche, which is like rock in case you're not familiar with Texas soil conditions. Pounding in a wooden picket-type sign holder is really difficult and the cost for wood versus wire was not that much of a bargain, all things considered. Costs for signs vary and calling around to get estimates is a good idea. For some voters, it's important to include the name of your sign printer, however small the type, so they can see that you used a local printer for your signs; it shows that you support the city's economy.

Those who print yard signs can be very helpful with color choices and designs. You have to bear in mind that yard signs are read in the few seconds that it takes to drive past them and so if you put too much information on them using print that is too small they can't be read.

It's interesting to me that some folks will put up anybody's sign and some people actually collect campaign signs. They will take them and may or may not display them but like to keep them in their garages. What for? I have no idea, but they do!

As noted previously, displaying a campaign sign is not necessarily an indication that the family inside the house will vote for that candidate, so when campaigning do not be deterred by a yard sign. You can always say, "I see your sign, but I would like to just give you some information about me. Thank you very much."

Often in elections, candidates accuse each other of vandalizing their yard signs, and while I suppose that it happens, many yard signs are run over by kids on bikes or are blown over by wind. Before placing a yard sign, you need to know your city's sign ordinances. In Leon Valley, signs may not be placed in public right-of-way, nor can they be placed on private property without the owner's permission.

Simple Things Nobody Tells You about Campaigning

If you wear sunglasses while campaigning door to door, take them off when chatting with people who answer your knock even if you have to squint. Some folks think that people who have on sunglasses don't want to look them in the eye and so must be not quite honest.

Wear sunscreen and a hat and carry water and sports drinks in a cooler if you have to campaign in Texas heat. I was on my last street for the day during one campaign when the heat began to get me. I had consumed all of my water and was getting red in the face and sweaty in the brow, not to mention a bit weak in the knees. And then I learned how truly kind some people can be when two of our fine Leon Valley citizens, whose houses I had already visited, came running down the street, one with a jug of Gatorade and the other with an icy-cold wet towel which I was told to keep. I don't know when I enjoyed the end of a campaign session more. It is so rewarding to know that the world is full of really nice people.

A fanny pack is a handy container for handouts as you go door to door. It leaves your hands free for a clipboard that's holding your walk list and the pen to make notes about the people to whom you have spoken. You can refer to your notes when you start calling them back to get out the vote on election day. You'll have points of reference and you can say something about the conversation you had with the voters you have visited.

If nobody is home, leave a handwritten note saying, "Sorry I missed you" on your campaign literature that indicates you have been there and that the campaign material wasn't just dropped at their doorstep by somebody else. I often commented on the person's garden or some architectural feature of the house so that the reader of my note knew that I was there personally.

You really do meet some interesting people on the campaign trail and you get to see neighborhoods and other areas that you normally might not drive to unless campaigning. It's good to remember that after you are elected you owe these people — at the very least — a drive-by occasionally to see how things are going in their neighborhoods and to see if you need to report any necessary repairs to the Public Works Department or other problems to other departments. (Actually, as noted elsewhere in this book, it's best to report problems to the city manager who then tells the department heads what needs doing.) Follow up is a fair way to say "thank you" for somebody's vote.

What Is the Worst Part of Running for Office?

For some of the respondents there was no "worst part" because they enjoyed campaigning. Having to make speeches was the worst part of campaigning for some people who thought that they were not good at speeches but preferred talking one-on-one with prospective voters. And while they liked meeting the citizens in door-to-door campaigning, it was physically tiring to walk a whole city.

One respondent said the "craziness that surfaces during campaigns" was the worst part of running for office — untrue rumors and information that gets circulated and can almost never be corrected, no matter how you try.

Another said it was the calls at home, especially when you are tired from walking door-to-door and have just plunked your aching body down on your favorite chair with or without a cold beverage.

I remember calls with rumors that were so unsettling. The person would call and say, "I know you don't want to hear this, but . . ." and I wanted to say, "If you know that I don't want to hear it, why are you telling it to me?" But you need to listen anyway because the information might indeed be useful in the campaign.

Voter apathy was the worst part of campaigning for many of those who responded; also the general lack of knowledge about local government. Many emphasized that they would like to get more people to vote; that some voter turnouts are "pathetic" and that "it's a sad commentary that more people are not interested in having a voice in local government or at least finding out what is going on." One respondent speculated that maybe if it were more difficult to register or if it had a price/cost perhaps more people would value their right to vote and use that right.

Dealing with questions about controversial issues while campaigning was difficult for many people. It's easy to voice an opinion but what if you don't have *all* of the facts about an issue? All you can do is answer to the best of your knowledge and then try to get more information about these issues before you go out campaigning again. I think it's better to be honest and lose votes than to dance a political two-step around issues. It's interesting that if you try to remain neutral about controversial issues, many people will say that you are indecisive, and that can lose as many votes as having the "wrong" opinion!

One big-city candidate with a district of about 165,000 citizens said it was difficult to reach everyone with information and cost a great deal of time and money. It should be noted that even in small cities, small districts of cities, and school boards, it still is difficult to reach everyone. Some people automatically throw out all campaign literature without reading it; some folks don't read newspapers; some just don't care.

And, again, some people are so angry at the federal or state government that they paint everyone in politics with the same brush. Please note that nowhere in this book have I used the word "politician" in the text unless some editor has put it in and I have missed it in the final draft. I just got tired of some people considering that word to be synonymous with deceit, trickery, and self-serving attitudes. To be sure, there are some people in public office who are there for the wrong reasons and do deceive, trick, and serve their own causes. But the vast majority of the people I met across the state and locally were sincerely trying to do some good for their communities at great cost of time, energy, personal life, and personal finances.

If you could wave a magic wand, what would you change about the election process?

One respondent said "it's a good and fair process as it is now . . . wouldn't change a thing." Three others agreed that nothing needs changing and another wasn't sure what if anything should change.

Candidates applauded the change in Texas law that allows a city to cancel an election if none of the candidates are opposed; it saves the city money and makes sense. Some respondents in cities with term limits wished that they would be abolished. "Term limits are detrimental to running a billion dollar business," said one big-city respondent. The other viewpoint is that term limits help get rid of the GOBS. Sometimes term limits may get rid of GOBS but then the GOBS will back their own GOBLETTES whom they control and so you really haven't changed anything in a GOBS city.

A small-city respondent said that in a small town, single member districts have "hurt the process and cause a narrow focus" on city problems instead of focus on the benefits to the whole city. My observation is that this is also a big-city problem, especially when dividing funds fairly for each district.

One respondent wished that the campaign time for both primaries and general elections would be shortened. Another wished that cities would have only biennial elections so that there wouldn't be the chaos of campaigns every year. Another wished that two-year terms could be extended to four-year terms. Also, there was a wish to establish filing fees or petition requirements for candidates in a general-law city* that doesn't have them. Some favor winning an election with a majority vote (where there is a run-off election if no one candidate gets a greater number of votes than the others) instead of only a plurality vote (where a candidate can win with only one vote).

One respondent said that city ethics committees should take complaints from city elections more seriously and deal with them in a more timely fashion. Another wished that the "politics could be taken out of politics" to make elections a positive process in which there would be no criticism of other candidates and no mud-slinging. Amen, I say to that!

---

*Texas cities can choose one of two forms of government: General Law, in which the city operates under the general laws of the State of Texas, or Home Rule, in which the city operates under a charter which can include laws in addition to the general laws of the state. In this case, a Home Rule city's charter could include a law requiring filing fees and/or petitions for candidates.

Many respondents would like a better way to finance campaigns. Nobody likes to ask for money but in large cities, in counties and other governments, few candidates can totally finance a campaign from private funds.

Some people wished that there were more public forums so more people could become acquainted with all of the candidates and their positions on issues, including candidates' special agendas. Some respondents wished that campaign times were shortened. One respondent said there should be no campaigning — only one night for all citizens to meet the candidates and decide the one for whom they will vote.

Low voter turnout is "disheartening" to almost all of the respondents. One respondent wished that there could be put into place "some mechanism which would assure that at least 50% of the registered voters could vote." Another said, "I'd require everyone to vote and be involved." One respondent wrote that we need to get more people involved and voting, and that perhaps it should be possible to vote from your home through the internet. One said we need more people to run for office in addition to more people voting and taking interest in local government.

One respondent summed up the voter apathy issue by saying, "I would like to somehow make more people vote. I think it's a sad commentary that more people are not interested having a voice in our local government or at least finding out what is going on." One respondent speculated that perhaps people who don't vote should be fined, and noted that this is done in Belgium. Lucky for me, I have friends in Belgium and so I emailed them to verify Belgian non-voting fines. My friend said that in Belgium voting is an obligation, ruled by laws. And indeed if you don't vote without having a valid reason, you will be fined. If you violate the voting law several times, you can go to jail. He said that a lot of people vote "in-valid, as a protest against the law."

My Belgian friend observes philosophically, "If you oblige people to do something, automatically a huge percent is against. If you don't, automatically a huge percent has 'other, better, nicer' things to do on such a [voting] day. And those who lament are the first to protest on the streets if something is not working as they think it should."

Isn't it interesting that citizens the world over seem to have the same attitudes?

Chapter 5:

The Scary C-word — Change

C hange is often the key factor in campaigns — the slogans call for changes in people, changes in policy, or just changes for the sake of change.

For many people change is a scary word. It means venturing out of your comfort zone and lurching uncontrollably into the great and terrible unknown. Fortunately, at least for some people, there are those who welcome change, embrace it, and take positive steps toward accomplishing it. Unfortunately, those who would cause change always have to deal with the CAVE people (Citizens Against Virtually Everything) who prefer either the status quo or want to return to the good old days. They have forgotten that most of the good old days are more old than good. They also forget that time, when it marches on, tramples those who do not march with the times.

When the subject of changing times comes up, I always think of one of my husband's colleagues who, when computers first entered our world, said they were just "a passing fancy" . . . a fad that would never last. When the year 2000 passed and computers certainly were no longer a passing fancy, he was asked if he had changed his mind about them. He thought a moment, and then said, "It's too soon to tell."

We all know such people — they build security fences around their comfort zones and throw away the key. Change is a cuss word. They don't want to change and don't want the people around them to do it either and they surely don't want changes in their city because "that's the way we've always done it here."

Remember Tevya, the head of his family in the musical *Fiddler on the Roof*, who said he was afraid that if he bent too far in accepting change he would break. People who fear change say, "If it ain't broke, don't fix it." They don't want to hear about preventive actions to take before something is "broke." And even when the GOBS who have always run the town, school board, or other entity, know in their hearts that change is inevitable they don't want it accomplished by the dreaded newcomer/outsider.

An old Texan once told me that "it's not how long you've been around but the roads that you've been dragged over." Experience has taught me that the old Texan was right. Age alone doesn't make us smart but being dragged over life's potholed gravel roads instead of primrose paths sure wears the edge off youthful idealism. Experience with my colleagues in public office, however, has revealed that no matter how you beat up on some people, they retain at least some of their idealism no matter how old they are or how rough the road to election is. And they continue to strive to do good things for their communities even when the rough road is uphill — and a slippery slope at that!

In my survey, I asked my colleagues to list what they thought were their greatest accomplishments, what changes they had made in their communities, the obstacles they faced in making changes, and how they overcame those obstacles.

My colleagues caused changes in their communities that ranged from introducing new technology to dealing with long-held, institutionalized intolerance. Mayors and councilmembers, county commissioners, judges, and school board trustees presided over building projects such as new libraries, new parks and park improvements, bridges, city halls and other city, county, or school facilities, water/sewer plants, road-building and street-improvements. They got street lights and traffic lights installed, began mailing monthly city newsletters, set up city web pages. Several were proud of environmental reforms such as promotion and institution of new programs for energy conservation, resource recovery, and recycling. Some started new programs for volunteer and employee recognition. Instituting programs that helped small businesses were also accomplishments. Some raised water/sewer fees to make needed improvements and some were instrumental in lowering fees and charges; some raised property taxes and some lowered them. Some officials had to deal with lawsuits; others found ways to get more grants from foundations and other funding sources. Still others were instrumental in bringing economic development to their cities, with new industry and downtown revitalization and more celebrations for their citizens that also bring in more tourists (and their dollars). Some had to deal with jail reforms and regulations. They worked to create new hospital and zoning districts and neighborhood preservation programs, to limit billboards and install landscaping in public areas. Several officials initiated beautification projects. One councilmember took city beautification to a new level by personally installing paneling in the city council chambers and other rooms in city hall, with the help of a willing spouse . . . certainly an extreme example of how public officials need their spouses' support to succeed in the job.

While most of the problems of small cities are the same as the problems of larger cities, the costs and effects on the general population seem to increase as the city population increases. The councilmember of a major city had to deal with a major problem of protecting the water supply for the city and surrounding area. Decisions about transportation, traffic control, water supplies, and many quality of life issues made by major cities directly affect the suburbs that surround them. However, the decisions by suburban officials can affect the quality of life in the major cities as well; flood control and transportation are good examples.

Often projects and plans become extremely controversial no matter how they are presented or needed. Some officials instituted city charter and campaign finance reforms, and various environmental controls that were not popular with businesses, community activists, and others in the community. One city official faced a backlash of bias and prejudice when trying to get a city swimming pool built. However, with patience, standing up to the GOBS, and a successful effort to gain public support, a swimming pool complex was built for all of the youth — black, brown, and white — to use and enjoy together. Changing such bias and prejudice has to be a laudable major accomplishment! When you grow up in the land of Archie Bunker-like prejudice, as I did, this councilmember's achievement made my heart skip a beat with joy.

Whenever I speak to a group about holding public office and someone asks me why anyone would want to do such a thing, I tell them that when you get a good idea, and you can get city staff, the council, and the public to help you make it work, and a whole lot of people benefit from the idea becoming reality, that is the greatest high you can possibly imagine and you will feel good all over again every time you remember the project.

Some officials made policy changes such as instituting long-range planning where it didn't exist. Two school board trustees were on their boards when corporal punishment was abolished in their districts and considered that policy change among their most memorable experiences in office. Changes in relationships with students' parents, better test scores, and better nutrition in cafeterias were also prized achievements for school board trustees. Policies that enhanced cooperation and harmony were achievements listed by another official. In times of controversy, my mentor and Leon Valley's Mayor Emeritus Ken Alley always said that "you can disagree without being disagreeable" and I was very fond of quoting him because I think that his advice is probably the best policy of all.

When People Disagree about Changes

Of course, you can't expect that everyone will agree or disagree without becoming disagreeable every time controversy rears its ugly head and loud voice. So what can you do when you have a really good idea and you need the help of others to make it a reality? According to the public officials who responded to my survey, *persistence* is the key that opens the door to change or to get any program or idea moving along. Patience is also a key word. *Persuasion, education,* and *organization* are also keys to making an idea into reality. Making change slowly sometimes defuses opposition. One respondent noted that fast change really "spooks people." In cities controlled by a Good Old Boys Society it helps to have the GOBS on your side.

Some respondents to my survey said that when you want to change something or do a project, it's best to exercise patience until

the timing is right. Government is a continual process, they say, so
you don't always have to stop and start over — you can build on
progress that has already been made. Others were able to get projects
going when there was spirited opposition by speaking to those who
were against the project on an individual basis. Some found it effective to describe the rationale behind proposed changes, listening to
the opposition's objections and then incorporating suggestions from
the opposition. Some advised winning the trust of the people by being
civil and fair. Some respondents got support from the public when
they stood up to the "old guard" because they believed the changes
were "the right thing to do."

One councilmember recalled that twenty-plus years ago dealing
with developers and new businesses was a major difficulty and occasionally the opposition was extreme. Developers and new businesses
didn't agree with the city's new viewpoint on zoning issues, special
use permits, landscaping requirements, and inclusion of handicapped
parking spaces in business areas. Builders didn't want to pay for sidewalks in subdivisions or conform to other city requirements. The
developers' lobby was very powerful during that city's period of rapid
growth. This councilmember's insistence and persistence regarding
the city's positions on building codes, landscaping requirements, and
other similar issues resulted in a threat of a shooting. The council
prevailed because it was united and persistent.

Problems with development are challenges and obstacles in many
communities. Sometimes councilmembers feel that developers' focus
on profit is in conflict with the future of the city and its needs. The
challenge is to get everyone to the table so that they can find common
ground. It helps if you can show that all citizens will benefit in some

way by the project, budget, issue, or solution to the problem.

When money is the problem that causes opposition, cities look for grants, loans, or other sources. Again, it helps if the majority of the citizens feel that they will benefit, which makes education and communication primary tools. However, one must be careful about certain terms. Once, during a campaign to enact an Economic Development Tax (EDT), a committee member said that the public needed to be educated about the EDT and then was criticized for implying that the citizens were "not educated" as in, without any education, deemed to be an insult. Some times, with some people, you just can't win.

A major obstacle for accomplishing any change, maintenance, or enhancement of existing things in a city, is apathy — apathy on the part of councilmembers, staff, or voters. Often the opposition has the loudest voice and so those who don't care enough and the apathetic become the enablers. Constant criticism from activist and other community groups and lobbyists can be a major obstacle to change and various other projects. Success in some cases was due to an office-holder's ability to organize the different factions so that they would work together to find a solution. Public or other opponents may change their attitudes if they have "ownership" in the project. It helps to keep your message in mind and to keep focused on your goal when you are dealing with opposing factions. You need to keep your cool even when dealing with those who criticize and complain but never pitch in to help or to offer a better way to do things, advises one respondent to the survey.

Getting various disparate groups and individuals to work together is always a challenge of leadership. It reminds me of two old and well-worn sayings:

A camel is a horse designed by a committee. ·

A committee functions best when only one member shows up at the meeting.

It is difficult enough to deal with opposition from CAVE people and GOBS, lobbyists, ordinary citizens, and other individuals and groups, but when the opposition is from your own council, you really have a problem and a challenge. Some councilmembers are very predictable and will always complain about cost (all costs are too high), or will have some other special "cause." This is especially true of one-issue candidates who campaign and get elected on one specific issue and then see every single item, plan, or project from one myopic viewpoint. Sometimes, city councils suffer from provincialism. They don't see that their cities are part of a region or state and they may not take advantage of organizations that can help them with education, training, expertise, and consulting. It's as if their cities are islands and totally independent from any neighbors. Parochialism/provincialism maintains the status quo, keeps the GOBS in power, and can prevent progress or inception of new ideas. When a city council seems stagnant or if councilmembers don't cooperate with each other to help the city progress, the key word again is patience, according to many elected officials. The advice from some of the respondents and people I have asked at various regional and state meetings is very simple: Endure and wait for the next election time; then work toward a change of leadership.

When You're the New Kid on the Block

The suggestions of patience and perseverance seem to be wimp factors in leadership to some people. Sometimes a newcomer to public office who is hell-bent on causing change behaves like the proverbial bull in a china shop. This is true in business and in other volunteer and professional organizations. My favorite memory about the aggressive approach when you are the newbie in the community comes from my experience of keeping African cichlids in my aquarium.

African cichlids are very aggressive and territorial fish. In a home aquarium, you have to provide caves, corners, and other places for them to reign in their own small domains. When you add a new fish you have to totally disorient the entire community by rearranging everything in the environment so that all fish have to establish new territories. This is a good idea with all fish but imperative with the African cichlids. Also, as with all aquariums, new fish must be the same size as the existing fish; smaller ones will be eaten — and that also may be a lesson for would-be officeholders.

One day I found a very pretty *Haplochromis burtoni* of the right size to add to my collection and it was not the usual high price. It was alone in a tank, but I was assured that it was alone because it was new and had just finished its quarantine and could be sold. I took Burt home and followed the usual procedures for adding a new fish to the aquarium. Burt, the newbie, immediately chased after every fish in the tank, chewing their tails, fins, and generally being disruptively aggressive. I turned off the lights and assumed that Burt and the others would settle down. The next morning when I looked into the tank, Burt was in a corner at the top of the tank, his tail and all his fins were shredded. Apparently the other fish had ganged up on him. And it got worse. They didn't let him feed on a regular basis and he never got to establish a nook of his own in the tank. Eventually he died.

Obviously, the lesson here is if you are the newbie in the community, don't chew everyone's tail or they will gang up on you. Think again about patience and persistence. And you might also remember that the owner of the tail that you chew may one day chew your tail, especially after the lights go out and folks outside of the tank can't see what's going on.

Waving a Magic Wand to Make Change

One question on the survey was; "If you could wave a magic wand, what would you change about your city?" Only one person responded to this question with "Nothing."

Respondents from all size cities and counties, and school district officials shared similar wishes such as more money to operate and to have higher educational levels for citizens. Educating every child was a school district priority and some city and county officials believed that higher educational levels would enable citizens to better understand issues before they made judgments about them.

Along with more money was a related wish to have more commercial areas, more downtown businesses, more high-paying jobs, increased population, and more growth space in smaller landlocked cities. While growth is desired by one entity for economic development reasons, it can be an economic problem for another. For example, growth in school districts means more new schools and so one respondent wished that cities would pay for traffic control — lights, signs, etc. — when new schools were built instead of requiring the school districts to pay for them.

Near the top of the magic-wand wishes was to change the level of the public's involvement in government. One respondent said that public apathy is a "silent enemy" and more people need to get involved. Another lamented that 90% of that city's residents were not involved in city matters. Greater participation by citizens in the electoral process and greater knowledge of how local government works was the wish of one city mayor. Another official wished to wave a magic wand that would make special interest groups more honest and yet another wished that the city could get rid of those who complain and criticize but never pitch in to help.

Most of those who responded to the survey wished to wave a magic wand to complete or initiate beautification programs for residential and business districts. In the opinion of one respondent, the city's business district was an "eyesore" and if magic could happen it should totally redo the business district and make it an "attractive, inviting place to drive though and to shop." Another wished for a magic wand to beautify the city, make it green, eliminate big signs, and keep it friendly.

Some wished they could get rid of old abandoned houses and certain apartments, and one wished to make changes in subdivisions that were platted and "abandoned by the developer" before the city was incorporated. Some would wave their wands to change policy such as formulating a strategic plan for protection of drinking water sources via natural areas and conservation easements. Others would change city land-use restrictions to require a greater percentage of green space and greater setbacks. Some needs were succinct: Wave a magic wand and get another bridge, build a major convention center, and have shorter meetings. While one respondent wished to restructure city hall buildings, another wanted to restructure city government so there would be no city manager.

And finally, one respondent from a suburban city wished to improve the relationships between the business community and the city and to get the business community to recognize the actual city as their locations' descriptions instead of just giving the street names in their advertising with no reference to the suburban city at all. (Note: In the San Antonio metropolitan area, people and businesses don't always know where San Antonio ends and the twenty-five suburban cities begin, despite the posting of city limits signs.)

One thing is certain, it takes more than a magic wand to cause change and my observation is that there are two basic philosophies that apply:

Method One: Method One is that you make changes subtly, bit by bit, with small steps taken on tiptoe so that nobody notices that change is happening. It's painless as it happens, and if the change is for the good, by the time anyone realizes that things are indeed different, the benefits are obvious and you don't have to go through all sorts of verbal sparring, political combat, and complicated compromises. If the action or policy is not as much of a benefit to everyone as originally thought, you may be able to go back to the way things were as quietly as you made the change.

Method Two: The other method to accomplish change, the bull-in-the-china-shop method, is more Machiavellian. You get rid of your opposition anyway you can such as defeating elected officials in bitter and mud-slinging campaigns that destroy their credibility and reputations, firing paid staff who have the audacity to point out flaws in your ideas, and terminating tenures of volunteers on boards and commissions who may have been appointed by your opposition. This can be divisive and risky and is certainly a rocky road to travel, but it does work faster than Method One. Also, there may be times when this approach is needed — for example, when the house really needs serious cleaning up — but you'd better be very sure that you are right about the need or someone will get you as you got someone else.

It seems to me that the method you choose depends upon what you think needs to change, how much of a political gambler you are, and what the mood of the populace happens to be at the time you decide to take action. Also, your personality can determine which method you can use effectively: Some folks believe that you catch more flies with honey than vinegar and know how to spread honey neatly; others always carry a hammer and always find nails to pound wherever they go.

Converting to Xeriscape

How many times this summer during the drought, did you make a resolution that you were going to replace all your St. Augustine grass with xeriscape?

Now is the time to fulfill your resolution. If you xeriscape now, it will mean that in the next drought, even if there are water restrictions, your landscape will prosper despite the weather conditions.

You can make your own xeriscape plan or enlist the help of your favorite nursery or landscape architect. Most nurseries offer the xeriscape conversion brochure for $5 which includes a step-by-step guide on how to plan and accomplish the conversion.

TAKE YOUR TIME

Most of us have budget limitations, so don't worry about planting everything at once. Plant what you can and cover the soil with mulch as you go along. Three or four inches of shredded brush mulch - which you can get free from the city's brush site (1800 Bitters) or have delivered for a reasonable price - can fill the space between plants until they can grow larger, or until you complete the planting.

HARDSCAPES ARE IMPORTANT

Don't forget patios and other hardscape areas. If you use permeable materials such as brickwork without mortar, flagstone, or decomposed granite, tree roots will prosper. Fall is the best time for planting shrubs, trees, and other xeriscape plants.

Here are some recommendations for xeriscape selections in a variety of sizes:

GROUND COVERS

Replace lawngrass with groundcovers. You can kill lawngrass sod now, before it goes dormant, with systemic herbicides like Round-up or Finale. Then after about two weeks you can plant the groundcover right into the killed sod. If you don't want to plant directly into killed sod, add 3-4 inches of compost and till the compost into the mix.

The traditional low-water use groundcovers are Asiatic jasmine and/or 'Katy' ruellia for sun or shade. Other groundcovers to consider are prostrate rosemary, iris, daylilies, and spreading juniper for full sun. In the shade use monkey grass, English ivy, or Texas Gold columbine.

LOW BORDERS AND SMALL SHRUBS

For the second level of plants, use perennials. In the shade, Turk's cap, ginger, shrimp plant, and tropical giant spiderlily work well. Salvias and lantanas are great for the sun.

Hollies and nandinas are the basic xeriscape shrubs. They work in sun or shade and are available in any size you need from ground cover to small tree. Dwarf yaupons, burford hollies, 'Gulf Stream' nandina, and standard nandinas are the best foundation shrubs.

LARGE SHRUBS AND SHADE TREES

Use Texas mountain laurel, pomegranite, ceniza, xylosma, loquat, ornamental pear, crepe myrtles, and redbuds for large shrubs and small trees. Xeriscape shade trees include Live Oak, Texas Red Oak, Mexican White Oak, Cedar Elm, and Chinese Pistache.

LEON VALLEY CIVIC AND BUSINESS A[...]
SPRING 1999 BUSINESS & NEIGHBORHOOD XERISC[...]

WHY: To encourage businesses and residents to plant trees and fl[...] to make Leon Valley a leader in xeriscaping as it has in [...] concept of Leon Valley as a residential community. Neig[...] neighborhoods and to encourage xeriscaping in new on[...]

WHO: All businesses and residents of all subdivisions in Le[...]

WHAT: FRONT YARDS ONLY. Bexar Master Gardene[...] conserving landscape designs, use of drought resist[...] landscaping or fix-up/face-lift beautification pro[...]

WHEN: Nominations will be accepted through Thursd[...]

HOW: You may obtain information at City Hall or b[...]

1. Give the name, address, and phone number of the [...]

2. Write a brief description of why the award should be given. List [...] possible. Photos are helpful but not mandatory. If applying for a spe[...] landscape/fix-up, supply "before" and "after" photos.

3. Mail or submit this form to the City of Leon Valley ATTENTION: Beautification Awards, Le[...] Valley Civic & Business Affairs Committee, 6400 El Verde Road, Leon Valley, Texas 78238. You may also fax this form to Felicia at 684-6988.

MASTER GARDENERS A MAXIMUM OF 100 POINTS USING THE CRITERIA BELOW.

- Planning and design (possible 20): Balance of element; creative use of hardscape (walkways, paving, etc.); harmony with architecture (graduation of plant height, unity of design, plant spacing, plant positions relative to windows, curbs, walkways)
- Soil Improvement (possible 10)
- Use of turf (possible 20): Reduction of turf area, amount of turf, type of turf
- Mulch/Groundcover (possible 20): Type and depth of mulch
- Plant material (other than turf) (possible 20): Low water demands, color use, esthetic effect
- Maintenance (possible 10): Turf mowing, weeding, fertilization

Participant's Phone # _____

Participant's Name _____

Participant's Address _____

Comments _____

(attach extra sheet for additional comments)   SIGNATURE (nominee or person nominating)

Chapter 6:

Tried and Succeeded, Tried and Failed, Tried Again

Often, turning an idea into a reality is like riding a rollercoaster — you get a rush going uphill, you get a feeling of losing your insides going downhill, and a lot of the time you feel like screaming. But when the ride is over, and you see that you haven't upchucked, fallen out of the gondola, or done anything else to embarrass yourself, you feel really exhilarated. Of course, if you have upchucked, fallen out of the gondola, or embarrassed yourself, exhilarated is not the word. You will probably feel pretty beaten up, squashed, disappointed, discouraged, and maybe angry — I mean, as in "mad as hell" with a desire to punch somebody, at least verbally.

Punching, verbally or physically, doesn't usually help anything. After a failure, you don't need to make more enemies. One thing is certain, you have to wait until you calm down and then self-talk your heart and ego back up to the functional level so that you can look for another ride — like bumper cars, or a pseudo airplane that spins you around and upside down. For reasons that defy all logical explanations, you can't resist starting all over again. Bear in mind that in politics, even if you try to take the easy way and ride the merry-go-round, you aren't likely to ride comfortably in one of the sleighs; you have to bob up and down on a slippery fake horse. Chances are that, being an optimist, you will probably get back on the rollercoaster! Remember what your Type A parents and teachers told you when you were a child: If at first you don't succeed, try, try again. I recall a seminar speaker who insisted that there is no such thing as "failure", only "lessons." I like the thought, but in reality, I think that while failure can be a "lesson," it's still a failure and you deal with it by getting on with the next challenge.

Unlike carnival rides, where you can see the end of the experience, when you embark on a project while in public office you can't always tell what the end result will be and how a current project will affect future endeavors. Times change, people's attitudes change, and you change too because you can't help but be affected by your experiences.

But no matter what happens, I believe that most people in politics are optimists. Otherwise why would reasonable, rational people willingly, and sometimes at great sacrifice of time, energy, and money, subject themselves to judgment and criticism by other people who may or may not be always reasonable and rational?

One thing is certain: After you have been in office for a while, you learn that sometimes you win and sometimes you don't. Sometimes, things work out better than you could have imagined; sometimes things won't work no matter how hard you try; and sometimes obstacles are placed before you that you couldn't possible foresee.

Often special interest groups dominate when an issue or project is presented and their dominance confirms the validity of the old saying that the squeaky wheel gets the oil. Those who shout loudest and longest can win, especially when there are so many people who are apathetic or who make little or no effort to become informed about complicated issues and projects. It's even more frustrating when the apathetic or ill-informed people are your fellow officeholders on your city council, board, or commission.

When the ill-informed people are reporters, newspapers become another huge source of frustration because once a story with errors gets printed it's almost impossible to get the correct information before the public. I remember the nuns in my elementary school saying that once you tell a lie or pass on gossip, it's like climbing to the top of a high tower, opening a feather pillow into the wind, and letting the feathers fly where they may. You can never, ever, gather up all those feathers again no matter how hard you try. That's certainly what happens when an erroneous news story is published or an erroneous public statement is made.

Another frustration is that even after you respond to a complaint, sometimes the complaining citizen is still not satisfied because the response was not fast enough. It should be noted that even elected officials have to face the bureaucracy of other governmental entities. City officials often have to cut through the red tape of the county, state, and federal departments and agencies, which can be far more tangled and knotted than most people know. Sometimes there just isn't enough money in the budget to solve a problem, and a complaint must be given a priority — possibly a much lower priority than the complaining citizen wants.

Sometimes it seems that the same problems, the same criticisms, the same challenges continue no matter how hard you try to do the right thing. It's frustrating when you have to make decisions based on "the big picture" — meaning how the decision will affect your city, county, or school district fifteen or twenty years from now and how that decision will benefit most of the people, not just the 35 or 135 or so people who are standing in the meeting chamber shouting at you and demanding that their wishes be granted right now. It takes courage to vote for what is best for the majority of people and to look into the future but these factors must be considered each time you vote, even if it means that you won't get reelected.

In my survey, I asked my colleagues about their frustrations and if there were times when they felt that all their efforts to run for office and work were just a waste of time; also, what were their greatest frustrations, regrets, or disappointments while in office. Some said they felt frustrated every week and others said they never felt that they wasted their time and effort and that each problem was a challenge to be overcome. I suspect that the answer to the "waste of time" or frustration questions depended on how things were going for them on the political rollercoaster at the time they filled out the survey form.

One person noted that often the amount of time spent waiting for colleagues to get organized seemed like a waste of time but on balance it was not. Several people felt that public service wasn't a waste of time, but the time it takes to get through city, state, and federal bureaucracies was extremely frustrating and that government needs streamlining. Some said that at times it seems projects will never be completed because it takes so long to "work the system." Delays because of bureaucracy can run up costs of projects too, and many times delays are also caused by the need to get those with different opinions to compromise. Another said that in eighteen years of office only one experience felt like a waste of time and that was when the governing body nearly got run out of town for trying to bring a state-of-the-art sophisticated sludge refining system to a town that didn't want it. Bringing in progressive new ideas is always a challenge.

Frustrations with people abound. Many expressed frustration over the public's apathy and lack of interest, especially on vital issues; or when the opposite is true — when small special interest groups get irate if they don't get their way. Another frustration is with chronic complainers who, even when their problems get solved, complain that the solution wasn't fast enough. One person said that it was difficult to get used to hearing complaints from people who always complain but refuse to contribute any positive solutions or personal time and effort to work toward a solution. Zoning cases frustrated some city officials, such as getting lobbied by people with pending zoning cases or not being able to get one's message understood in controversial zoning cases.

There are frustrations with colleagues when one tells the other to stop asking questions or makes unjust personal critical remarks during a discussion. Or when a colleague refuses to give up a previously held viewpoint no matter how much information proves that viewpoint erroneous. Worse yet, when a new council comes on board and criticizes everything the previous one did without bothering to find out why they did it out-going officials wonder if they wasted years of their lives to no avail. In fact, constant criticism no matter how much good has been accomplished, along with gossip and untruths in the media, are a major source of disappointment and frustration to many elected officials. Getting information to the public so that voters understand issues is difficult enough without having the issues distorted by misinformation in the press.

Getting bashed by newspapers was another frustration, especially when an official feels as if all the good that has been accomplished is overshadowed by the reason for the bashing. It is especially upsetting to have a front-page story in a newspaper about a controversial public issue include exposure of a public official's personal life mistakes and/or skeletons in the family closet.

Trying to get others to see the big picture and revisiting the same problems and challenges every year made at least one official wonder if time was wasted being in office. Getting others to accept fiscal responsibility was a problem for another person. The need for more money for projects in anti-tax times is a constant challenge for any officeholder and nobody likes to have politics interfere with the way in which issues are resolved or left unresolved.

Often one leaves office before certain significant projects have been completed, which is a major frustration for many elected officials, especially where term limits have been imposed. However, the greatest frustration of all is not getting reelected when you really believe you have done your best for your city, board, commissioners' court, or state house. And this frustration is compounded if you lose by small margins, as one state office candidate did by 99 votes, as one city council candidate did by 12 votes, and a mayoral candidate by 1 vote.

The good and encouraging news to any would-be political office candidate is that while many officeholders have regrets about one decision or another, after all is said and done, most really believe that the good times and feelings of accomplishment outweigh the frustrations and disappointments. Almost all said persistence is the key to getting things done.

Here are some of my own experiences during my four years on council and six years as mayor. While they took place in Leon Valley, Texas, they could have happened anywhere. I hope that my pitfalls and pratfalls will help someone who is attempting similar projects.

Sometimes You Win Despite Obstacles

Xeriscape Is Not Zero-scape

Our city had a "Beautification Contest" in which several people, who were friends of the mayor or councilmembers, would give a first, second, and third prize for landscaping to three chosen businesses on our city's main street. Winners would get a sign to proudly place amidst their shrubbery. It was considered a way to encourage businesses to spruce up their frontages. The same people seemed to win each year and there were no discernable criteria other than that the area would be clean, neat, and have some plants.

The first year that I was on the council, our city sponsored a xeriscaping workshop. Xeriscaping was just beginning to be publicized as a means of having a nice yard but without draining the Edwards Aquifer which is the primary water source for our area. Droughts are frequent in South Texas, and during drought and water rationing yards go brown and flowers are a luxury. Why not have a xeriscape program and encourage beautification with water-saving native plants and water-saving landscape designs for homes as well as businesses?

The first obstacle was a need to explain xeriscape since many folks thought the only drought-resistant plants were cacti. Another obstacle was to get people to replace water-needy grassy lawns with mulched planted areas. It helped that we had an annual environmental program, now called Earthwise Living Day, in which to distribute information about xeriscapes. I liked the motto "Xeriscape is not

ZEROscape" which played upon most folks' mispronouncing the word "xeriscape" as "zeroscape" and which made people think that xeriscape was zero landscaping. The motto never impressed anyone but I persisted . . . and it still never impressed anyone.

I also tried to call the project a xeriscape *program* instead of contest but that concept never got going either; people are more accustomed to contests than to programs. I saw no need to have neighbors compete with each other and giving first, second, third meant that efforts of others were not rewarded. So we changed to giving Awards of Excellence and Merit based on a point system set by the Bexar County Master Gardeners, who volunteered to judge the yards.

To get the program started in the neighborhoods we gave awards very liberally during the first two years; the Master Gardeners were asked to be generous with their points. As the program grew, criteria were more realistic. The program grew rapidly when folks saw that they could have traditional landscape designs with native plants while saving on their water bills and their own energy in the summer. Decreasing turf means less time mowing! It helped that a new subdivision promoted xeriscapes that were exemplary.

An unexpected obstacle was the yard of a prominent family which almost killed the whole program. The family lived on a well-traveled street in their subdivision and had received awards for a "wildscape" in the first two years of the program when judges were more lenient. The wildscape by the third year was truly wild with bushes encroaching on the sidewalk forcing people to walk in the street, and according to some people who called city hall, the wildscape presented the general appearance of abandoned property. People called to complain and to say that "If that is xeriscaping, I don't want it!"

But every now and then, a blind hog gets lucky and finds an acorn, and our program got lucky, too. Our very visible park monument was xeriscaped as an Eagle Scout project by a couple of our city's Boy Scouts and it was a super, professional-looking job. Native plants bloom during all seasons and the xeriscape project was shown in a public television documentary. People copied the plant choices and proper use of mulch and the program grew so that almost every street had at least one xeriscape front yard. By the sixth, seventh, and eighth years, the committee, run by a super dedicated volunteer Master Gardener, had 80 to 100 or more entries annually. Some subdivisions took pride in the numbers of entries that they had. We did learn to put the year of the award on the yard signs because sometimes winners would move and then new people would let the yard go wild. (Even a xeriscape or wildscape needs some taming every now and then.) We didn't want a repeat of the wildscape problem. Then a new administration, which didn't know or ask why we put a year on the award sign, wanted to eliminate the year designation so signs could be reused. Another lesson: When you are the new administration, find out the "whys" before you make change.

Revising a Sign Ordinance

Leon Valley is totally surrounded by the City of San Antonio and does not have a traditional "downtown." Instead, most of its businesses are on Bandera Road, which is also Texas State Highway 16 and more or less cuts the city in half.

Strip malls line both sides of the road. Many are old, some were less than attractive (a politically correct way of saying they looked really bad), and many were cluttered with signs left behind by closed businesses. Temporary signs hung from permanent signs, and some of these were tattered and torn.

Every time we had a workshop to set city goals or to develop a city vision, the first criticism from citizens was that the city needed to "do something about Bandera Road." It looked cluttered, "junky," and "just plain ugly" or "like a third world country." Many people complained that there were so many temporary signs, flags, and banners that they couldn't even find the signs of the stores and businesses they wanted to visit. People also complained about garage sale signs left up long after the sale was over.

We had a sign ordinance but it was not proactively enforced due to lack of personnel and a traditional tolerance that some people claimed was beneficial to business. Surveys of citizens revealed that clutter from signs, lack of upkeep of existing signs, and general lack of neatness made them feel unsafe and made them think that businesses in such strip malls probably didn't have good products. Some business owners and others found that information unbelievable and thought that the status quo was just fine and that the proposed stricter sign ordinance would cost businesses too much money, and not having a lot of temporary signs would prevent potential customers from learning about their sales and special services. Some councilmembers were opposed to a stricter sign ordinance.

Several workshops were held for citizens and business owners alike to explain how the ordinance would work. Money was found for a part-time person to enforce the new sign ordinance, and after numerous compromises council passed the ordinance, allowing for an amortization period for businesses to conform to the new requirements. The effect was immediate. Bandera Road looked better, cleaner, and people noticed.

I believe it was a major achievement and a step in the right direction toward making Leon Valley's business district look like a place to do business. The next step would be to pass a tree/landscaping ordinance but I also believe that you can't take too many steps at one time. If you want people to dance with you, and you have stepped on their toes during the two-step, you need an intermission before you ask them to tango or waltz when you might tread on their toes again.

I should add a bit of reality here. After a subsequent election, some newly elected GOBS councilmembers deemed the sign ordinance to be anti-business and began to water down some of the restrictions. But those of us who tried know that we at least made an effort to make the business areas more attractive.

Sometimes You Lose
The Great Unfunded Mandate

Elections aren't the only times when folks polarize over what the city should do, and occasionally something that seems so rational to elected boards and city councils gets everyone totally riled up beyond any level that one can comprehend. Worse yet, sometimes a project fails and that failure spills over on future efforts in the form of citizen distrust of the decision-makers. And, although it is unfair, transgressions by people in other entities — school boards, city, state, or federal — spill over on all of us, and no matter how honest, dedicated, and sincere we may be, we all get painted with the same "guilty" scarlet letters.

In our city, in my opinion, our first effort to comply with an unfunded federal mandate called Stormwater II was the type of failure that spilled over on future city efforts. It was more like a storm surge that really rocked the boat in the form of citizen protest.

When the EPA (Environmental Protection Agency) came out with Stormwater II regulations (an unfunded mandate from the federal government dealing with environmental issues regarding storm-water runoff), city leaders, city staff, and I saw that it was an opportunity to raise money for projects that would solve our city's flooding problems and which would clean up the environment as well. The annual cost to each household and business was reasonable — or so we thought. Oh, were we wrong!

Stormwater II became one of the most controversial issues in the six years that I was mayor. The public mood was one of "no more taxes and fees" and our presentation of the projects was unacceptable to the citizens for various reasons that would take too many pages and too much misery on my part to describe. The GOBS and CAVE people were joined by others who normally do not react negatively. And in my opinion, the Stormwater II controversy adversely affected our EDT elections (three failed) and a city election because it gave the GOBS and CAVE people a weapon to use against those who were in favor of Stormwater II. The weapon was: "They want to take our money and waste it" and the anti-Stormwater II campaign was extremely successful because the mood of the time was anti-tax and anti-fees. In my opinion, it also undermined confidence in city staff who presented the program and led eventually to the firing of the city manager.

The projects that would have been funded by Stormwater II fees would have been good for the environment and would have enabled the city to proceed with several flood mitigation projects. Oddly, the very people who would have benefited the most — those whose properties either were in flood plain or had been put into flood plain by the newest FEMA survey — were the most vehement objectors or were among the totally apathetic and disinterested.

At the core of what went wrong, I think, is that we assumed that the public would accept the idea for two reasons: 1. Our city had experienced two major floods, including water recently in areas that previously had not flooded. 2. Our city is an area leader in environmental matters, so we assumed that our environmentalists, especially, would embrace an environmental clean-up plan. They did not.

The rule of a productive life in politics and for any endeavor has always been, is now, and ever will be: *Never assume anything!* We broke that rule and failed.

My survey of other elected officials gave me consolation when I read about their frustrations when trying to bring new and extremely progressive ideas to their citizens. I was especially consoled by the story of the official who related an attempt to bring a sophisticated sludge-processing facility to the area that took sludge and refined it into methanol sulfur and inert road base. The opposition was so intense that they felt as if they were going to be "run out of town." I thought we would be run out of town, too.

It's times like these that dedicated, usually optimistic, elected public servants feel that all the effort to run and to work was a waste of time and effort and we wonder why we keep trying. But we do continue because sometimes you win!

Sometimes Everybody Wins
Los Leones Student Arts Festival

A conversation in a parking lot about the problems faced by artistic kids who get little encouragement to consider the arts as a career led to a successful small city/school district arts festival partnership that grows each year in participation and attendance.

Los Leones Student Arts Festival, a truly unique festival of visual arts, continuous entertainment, food, and fun, is presented as a partnership between the City of Leon Valley, Northside School District, and Northside Education Foundation.

Los Leones seeks to teach the "business of art" to arts students from elementary school and up. Students sell their works or prints of their works along with the works of invited professional artists. Prices are very affordable and prints are only $5. All artists give ten percent of their sales to Los Leones instead of a booth fee; funds are used to defray costs of the event. Admission is free.

A T-shirt design contest is held, students are given a "commission" with design criteria (Los Leones colors of blue, gold, and orange and a lion motif), and the winner's graphic design goes on the T-shirts and all promotional materials. All arts classes participate and the contest has been won by elementary as well as secondary school students. All design winners and runner-up winners receive cash prizes. More cash prizes and art-related gifts are given to students by honorary judges who make a "personal pick of the show." Judging is on the Friday evening before the show; students receive their blue ribbons and prizes from the judges in ceremonies held at the show. Even the student soloist who sings the national anthem at the beginning of the show gets paid.

In addition to teaching the business of art, Los Leones seeks also to encourage the arts and to provide a community fun event for all ages. Dance troupes, storytellers, jazz ensembles entertain continuously both inside and outdoors. Food booths are operated by various non-profit organizations; they pay a minimal food booth fee.

Community support for Los Leones increases each year. Los Leones has grown to participation by more than 40 Northside School District campuses, more than 25 judges, and attendance by about 2,600 people. The show fills two community center buildings, the porches outside of the buildings, and the sidewalks of the area. Sidewalk chalk art was featured in the most recent Los Leones and was a huge success; businesses sponsored the art teams by paying for supplies.

Los Leones is limited only by space, and the goal is that one day the show will have so many artists that they will be set up in the park across the street from the Leon Valley Community buildings. It is a success because of dedicated volunteers, city and school district staff. The best part of its success is that in nearly ten years, the only complaints have been a desire for more parking space, space for more artists, and more food booths. How often do you hear complaints requesting more of *anything*, much less requests for more of *everything?*

Aside from being an idea whose time had come, I think the success of Los Leones is due to its partnership with the Northside School District and Northside Education Foundation. The city had the venue and a committee of volunteers, the school district had the expertise and artists, the Foundation provided staff assistance and the 501c3 non-profit organization status which makes donations to Los Leones tax deductible. Partnerships really work!

Household Hazardous Waste Disposal Project

A councilman from a neighboring city and I deplored the lack of facilities for proper disposal of household hazardous waste —

batteries, paint, paint thinners, insecticides, fertilizers, and numerous other things which should not be thrown into the garbage for regular pickup because they harm the environment when they seep out of landfills.

Since our big city neighbor had a facility, we tried to make a deal with the big city for the smaller cities in our area. After two years of back and forth talks, we realized that we were looking in the wrong place for help. Waste disposal is a regional issue so we went to AACOG which held a workshop on how other cities dealt with hazardous household waste and provided information on companies that collect it. AACOG got grant monies to help pay for disposal for the cities which applied for the funding and for Bexar County which applied for funding to help people who lived in unincorporated areas of the county. After the initial funding cycle, AACOG and Bexar County worked together with the small cities to offer a program in which all of the residents of suburban cities of the metropolitan area and the unincorporated areas of the county could properly dispose of their hazardous household waste. Funding was obtained so that the disposal was free, which was even better.

This project was a success, I think, because small cities, which had no facilities partnered with the County, which had administrative staff that transcended city limits, and with AACOG, which had the expertise for finding the disposal company and securing the grant. It was an efficient use of grant monies for an important environmental project and benefit to citizens as well as the environment. Again, partnerships work.

Sometimes Everybody Loses
Economic Development Sales Tax

Politics abounds with ironies. One of my first years as mayor, with the help of city staff and the support of our council, the City of Leon Valley sponsored legislation that would allow small cities to enact a half-cent increase in the sales tax to be used for economic development. Previously, the state law allowed only cities with 200,000 and greater populations to hold elections for this purpose. We got support from our local governments in the Greater Bexar County Council of Cities and, most importantly, the Texas Municipal League and state legislators. After the legislation was passed, small cities across the State of Texas held elections, formed Economic Development Corporations and did great things for their cities . . . but not us. The City of Leon Valley failed to pass a sales tax increase for economic development — not once but three times.

When I testified before the legislative committee involved with this issue, I was so proud to be the mayor of the so very progressive and proactive city that was going to do wonderful things for the soft economies of small cities throughout the state. I felt like the Joan of Arc for Economic Development. And I can tell you that the first time you testify before a senate committee feels almost as intimidating as Joan's impending burning at the stake! The legislators sit on a dais that seems a full story higher than the desk at which those who testify sit. The legislators come and go during testimony and one wonders where they have to go and why they don't just sit there and listen to the trembling voices asking for their help.

I felt confident when the legislator who was supporting our bill came into the room and spoke in its behalf. Also I'd been told that if I didn't testify well, one of the TML lawyers would speak on our bill's behalf to make sure it got favorable exposure; there is comfort in knowing you have a backup.

The person who testified before me had come to ask for funding legislation, and when asked questions he messed up all the papers in his manila folder and couldn't find any answers at all. The legislators appeared annoyed. Two walked out. My confidence began to sag and I hoped that someone else would follow the disaster. I followed the disaster, took a deep breath, and said what I'd planned to say. Like all things that seem scary, it was nowhere near the traumatic experience I had anticipated. The legislators, who were people familiar to me, asked simple questions, to which I had answers, and in what seemed like thirty seconds, said "Thank You." And it was over.

The city manager and I went home from Austin feeling good about the reception we got and we reveled in the wondrous things that would happen in Leon Valley after our city passed the Economic Development Tax. We could attract new businesses that the people said they wanted when we had citizen workshops on the future of our city's economy; we would promote the businesses we already had which were small businesses that didn't have advertising budgets; we would stop the exodus of business to the newer areas of the county; and we would make our business district so appealing that those who normally drive through the city on State Highway 16 would be enticed to stop and shop. Leon Valley would not be one of the declining wagon-wheel suburbs being written about in the various government service publications.

We got how-to information about sales tax elections and followed the rules. I asked former mayors and other civic leaders to serve on the committee and just knew the people would see the benefits of a half-cent tax increase, about 85 to 90% of which, statistics showed, would be paid by shoppers from outside of the city. Property tax revenues would not need to be raised as often since our city budget would be enhanced when promotion of city businesses would yield greater sales.

The committee held workshops for citizens to explain the tax, did a mail-out explaining the tax, talked to people to explain the tax — in short, we explained the heck out of the tax . . . or so we thought. The opposition put up huge red signs that gave the first impression to people driving by that the sales tax would be raised *by* 8.25% instead of *to* 8.25% and convinced the business community that nobody would shop in Leon Valley if the sales tax went up. The opposition had no problem convincing the public to vote against the EDT because the mood of the day was anti-tax and so the anti-tax campaign was stronger than the pro-tax campaign.

The second time our city attempted to pass the tax, the new committee faced the same opposition as the first committee but an active door-to-door campaign gained more pro-votes than previously. Unfortunately, this committee ran into a wall created by GOBS and CAVE people that was unbelievable because some of the same people who were on the first committee joined the opposition, and the previous campaign's red anti-tax signs seemed tame compared to the opposition's slanderous red paper campaign flyers that brought up the Stormwater II fiasco as a historical fact about excessive money-grabbing attempts by city officials.

One of the great oddities of politics is that people can oppose an issue one time and then support it another. For some people, all elections are a game, to be won at any cost, and the issues or candidates involved are merely incidental to the game. I was told by a local kingmaker that you can't win unless you "go for the jugular," that you can use half-truths and outright lies and anything else that will get you a win. The kingmaker told me that the way to win is to get the voters angry about something or somebody — doesn't matter if the reason for the anger is fictitious, just that it's something that "gets them mad enough" to go to the polls and vote the way you want them to vote. Taxes make people mad, the kingmaker insisted, and if you can exploit that anger, you win and they lose no matter what the issue is.

When I said that personally I can't even play chess that way, much less formulate strategies that treat living people as pawns, I was told that I didn't have the right attitude and would never be a success in politics. Like the majority of people with whom I have worked, I respect the voters and take elections seriously. But every now and then you run into a kingmaker or someone who wants the Andy Warhol fifteen minutes of fame and these people can be formidable, especially if the mood of the people is anti-tax, anti-government, or just anti-any/everything.

The third time our city tried to pass the EDT we had a new committee, composed of some of the people from the first and second committees. It included some who opposed the EDT previously but who had changed their minds and a new chairperson who volunteered to work on the project. Unfortunately, some of the same people who opposed the first two attempts garnered more support, and more red papers were circulated as well as signs in businesses encouraging a NO vote. It is my belief that the seeds of distrust sown by the slanderous campaigns against Stormwater II, the second EDT election, and a particularly nasty city council election the same year as the second EDT election yielded a harvest of divisiveness and distrust, not to mention disgust from people who don't want to vote at all due to "dirty campaigns." I feared that it would be years before our city returned to the civility that existed prior to the red paper campaigns. Fortunately, I was wrong and the most recent election was civil and not negative.

I think everyone — the city, the businesses, the citizens — all lost the benefits that could have been gained had our city joined the other progressive cities in Texas which are renovating their cities' economies and keeping property taxes lower with activities sponsored and maintained by their economic development corporations. Some new business promotion plans have emerged and I hope that they will work; some of us never lose our optimistic attitudes, even after we leave office!

Sometimes You Think You've Won

Historical Preservation

Our city has an old stagecoach stop that was on a tract of land purchased by a company planning to build a motel on the part of the land elevated out of flood plain. The 1860s limestone buildings on the property included the two-story main house with a leaky roof and rickety porch, a smaller building thought to be the old kitchen in the days when kitchens were separate from the main houses, and a stacked-stone barn or shed — a rare type of structure in the area. Homeless people and others had vandalized the property which was privately owned but basically neglected after the last resident, the matriarch of a prominent family, died.

The house had a colorful history and was said to be haunted by "old man Huebner" which led to even more vandalism on Halloween. Trespassers especially sought Mr. Huebner's grave which was in the woods behind the property. Mr. Huebner, according to legend, enjoyed his spirits and was once locked up in the attic so that visitors wouldn't see him while he was extremely spirited. After the visitors left, the saying is that Mr. Huebner was found to be "either dead or dead drunk" and so they buried him on the property. His ghost was said to roam the upper floors of the main house at night, making all sorts of scary sounds.

Unfortunately for the history buffs, the buildings were on a part of the land that the motel needed for its parking lot. Negotiations with the motel management company were successful and the parking lot was placed elsewhere. However, after the word got out that the buildings might be torn down for a parking lot, and before the negotiations with the motel management began, the public became polarized. Some people wanted the buildings saved by the city at any cost. Some people thought the buildings were an eyesore that should be bulldozed. The vast majority wanted the buildings saved but not with public money that might be taken from street maintenance and other city services. I had phone calls and letters from all sides of the issue.

The solution seemed simple to me. I would ask the motel management people to donate the house and the land under it to our city's historical society, which was a non-profit organization with a "tax number," so that the historical society could restore the buildings with grants that were available for historical preservation and not available to cities. I would ask the historical society to accept the donation and since funding was not readily available, another councilmember and I would pay the liability insurance for two years. I personally pledged a total of $1,000, and have honored that pledge. I would put my money where my mouth was, as the saying goes. (Note that holding public office at no salary actually costs money.) The hotel people and the society agreed. The house and other buildings would be saved!

The motel management also agreed to sell the remaining land parcel of 36 acres, which was appraised at $650,000, to the city for $350,000. This land is adjacent to our city park, and since our city is more than 90 percent developed enlarging an existing park seemed to be a huge benefit to future citizens. How to pay for the land became controversial, with some people and councilmembers wanting to hold a bond election and others wanting to use existing funds from certificates of obligation borrowed by the city for public works projects. We would have to wait about four months to hold a bond election. In that time, the hotel might have sold the property to someone else, but most of all, there would be four months of divisive controversy that, in my opinion, would not be good for the city. The matter was brought before the council with three options available:

1. Use money from the General Fund Reserve, often nicknamed the "Rainy Day Fund" — money that must be in reserve for the city in case of a disaster or emergency. I didn't think it was appropriate to go into the reserve funds; to me, it would be like dipping into your family savings account to buy a new car when you didn't absolutely need one.

2. Hold a bond election. My feeling was that since, by law, it would be about four months until a bond election could be held, the different opinions of various groups would just intensify as time passed; it would be too divisive for the city.

3. Use funds that were available from certificates of obligation obtained by the city some years previously for public works projects. This was my choice for reasons noted above in #2. — the disadvantage of holding a bond election.

Leon Valley is a Type-A General Law City, which means that the mayor does not have a vote unless there is a tie vote. We have five councilmembers and so a tie occurs only when one councilmember is missing and the vote is two to two. Mysteriously, one councilmember was called out of town the night this matter came before council and the vote was two for a bond election and two for purchase with available funds. I have voted only three times in the six years I was mayor, and all of those times I made a whole lot of people mad at me. I voted for purchase with available funds. I went home feeling good because now the buildings were secure with the historical society and the land would belong to the city and we would all live happily ever after.

I was confident that the city, the council, and I had won a victory for the future. Later we held a charrette or collaborative planning session to determine best use of the 36 acres, but unfortunately funding was not available to implement the ideas that came from the charrette. However, the city still was a winner, the land was ours, and when funds became available, our park would be extended and we would all live happily ever after.

Oh how naïve can a person be! As this book is being written, the historical society has new leadership and that leadership has determined that the society should lease and hold all of the land and manage it, but the city should do some maintenance. The current city council has agreed and leased the land to the society. The legalities of such a partnership and possible liabilities in our litigious society are interesting to say the least, and the issue has again polarized some of our citizens. Also, there is concern that when focus on development of the acreage has priority, then there isn't enough attention, time, and money paid to the restoration of the historical buildings.

So sometimes you think you have won but the controversy returns and/or continues. Is there such a thing as a semi-win? Who knows? I do not.

Leon Valley Leadership Program

Conferences and seminars for public officials can be super sources for good ideas. After attending a session on a Leadership/Government 101 program elsewhere in Texas, a councilmember and I decided that our city should have one. That year, I gave each councilmember a challenge and the councilmember who attended the leadership program session with me was given the challenge to work with staff to start a program in Leon Valley. Fortunately for our city we had extremely professional staff and the program was set up so that citizens could attend sessions on six Saturday mornings. Each session featured a different city department and was hosted by that department — Police, Fire, Public Works, Administration, Development, Finance, with an opening session on City Government and Elected Officials Duties.

The pilot/first program was given for volunteers who already were on our city's boards, commissions, and committees. They were very enthusiastic about it and their only criticism is that they wished it could be longer. Participants said that they wished everyone in the city could take the program because it was so informative. Our city won a Community Program award from AACOG for this effort. The second year, the program had 21 participants and resulted in 21 very dedicated volunteers for the city's boards, commissions, and commit-tees, some of whom had never been active in the city before. Also, two of the participants ran for council. So the leadership program met its goal of getting informed citizens active in the city. We had to add to the number of people required for a couple of the committees because we had more volunteers than we had positions open — not the usual situation and a most encouraging result!

The word got out about the program's success and other cities asked if they could send their councilmembers and citizens to our sessions. Unfortunately we didn't have enough people sign up the third year and the decision was made to skip a year. Then the last program had about 12 participants, some of whom were already city volunteers but had not had the course. Almost all of the previous leadership program graduates were still on various committees; they

also were informed participants in special workshops held that year —
a vision workshop, a workshop to determine use of a land parcel
bought by the city, and a sign ordinance workshop.

The leadership course was a benefit to city staff even if it meant
extra work for them because they were able to show their expertise to
citizen/taxpayers who were all impressed by the competency and
professionalism of staff and departments. So the program was a
successful public relations tool as well as an educational event.
Another side effect was that city employees made an extra effort at
"housekeeping" to impress the participants, and the additional pride
from the compliments from the participants inspired them to maintain that level of extra neatness and order.

This project worked because our city staff had the expertise to
make interesting presentations about the way their departments function and we had a staffers who were skilled in facilitating workshops
and making the sessions fun as well as educational.

When I left office, all the boards, commissions, and committees
were composed of dedicated, well-informed citizens. After that year's
election, the new council and mayor decided to do a purge of the
previous council's appointees for political reasons so the city lost
many of the people it had trained to serve. The turmoil that followed
was an example of a significant lesson about use of power: Just
because you *can* do something, it doesn't mean that you *should* do it.
Also, when you want to make change, it's less traumatic if it's made
gradually. The bull-in-a-china-shop approach may clear the room but
the bull won't escape unscarred by the chaos! Also, people don't forget
their encounters with bulls — or just plain bull!

Community Leadership Program Graduates

"(The Community Leadership Program) gave me a personal connection with local government."
2002 Graduate

"I understand the way the City runs...I have a good respect for all city leaders and employees."
2001 Graduate

"(The Community Leadership Program) has given me a better understanding of the elective process, roles and responsibilities of city staff and elected officials."
2002 Graduate

"All (of The Community Leadership Program) sessions were very informative."
2001 Graduate

Graduates of the Leon Valley Community Leadership Program are involved. Today many are active on the City's various Boards, Committees, and Commissions.

Take the opportunity to be part of the solution. Apply to the Leon Valley Community Leadership Program!

What is the Leon Valley Community Leadership Program?

The City of Leon Valley presents an innovative approach to recruiting new community leaders.

Our City has developed a unique, hands on leadership training program, aimed at providing citizens with a working knowledge of the city.

There will be five sessions consisting of four hours each, to be held over an eight week period. Participants will learn about the basic roles and responsibilities of City Government as well as attend specific sessions covering the functional aspects of community and public safety, infrastructure and public improvements, budget and financial obligations.

Classes will be facilitated by elected officials, staff and invited guest speakers.

Participants must attend all five of the scheduled classes, plus one regularly scheduled City Council meeting and one Zoning Commission meeting.

Upon completion, graduates will be recognized at a future City Council meeting.

Leon Valley Community Leadership Program
"2001 Alamo Area Council of Governments' Regional Community Project of the Year"

LEON VALLEY
T E X A S

COMMUNITY LEADERSHIP PROGRAM
★ 2003 ★

The Community Leadership Program is an educational training program designed to inform citizens of the organizational and functional aspects of municipal government.

The Community Leadership Program will create an awareness of leadership opportunities in the Leon Valley community.

The Community Leadership Program is for current and aspiring community leaders.

The Community Leadership Program is for you!

... Honermann, Director
Community Development
(210) 684-1391 ext. 227 or
www.ci.leon-valley.tx.us

...MUNITY LEADERSHIP PROGRAM
ENROLLMENT APPLICATION
Please Print or Type

Date of Birth
Home Phone
Bus. Phone
TX Drivers License No.   FAX
...D   Yes ❑ No ❑   Name/Address of High School
...ree   Yes ❑ No ❑   Name/Address of College
Supervisor   Your Title
Telephone   Date Hired

...is Program.

...o night be   Subject(s) you are most interested in learning about
...ber: (Check all that apply):
                        ❑ Zoning   ❑ Fire Department
                        ❑ Platting   ❑ Library
                        ❑ Building   ❑ Public Works
                        ❑ Code Enforcement ❑ Parks & Recreation
                        ❑ Police Department ❑ Other

I hereby certify that there are no willful misrepresentations, omissions, or falsifications in the foregoing statements and answers to questions, I understand that any omission or false statement on this application shall be sufficient cause for rejection for enrollment or dismissal from the Program. I pledge the time commitment to attend.

Signature   Date

Sometimes You Think You've Lost
A Nasty Election and A Difficult Council

Sometimes things get truly ugly. The Good Old Boys Society decided to run and ruin an election with innuendos, flyers, and a downright nasty campaign. The local kingmaker whose tactics were described earlier in this chapter was the real winner in the election; the candidates supported by the kingmaker were incidental to the process but came on board with acrimony and antagonism. City staff was harassed constantly and the concept of disagreeing without being disagreeable was discarded. Everything became an issue from the budget to city hall office hours.

I was the primary target, and — amazing to me — one of my major faults was that I wouldn't violate the Texas Open Meetings Act by holding unposted meetings and calling councilmembers before our regular meetings to get their opinions about items to be on the agenda. One candidate (who won election) actually said, during a discussion about an issue, that we didn't have to bother with the open meetings act. I felt exonerated when the Texas Rangers were called in to investigate whether or not a violation occurred in San Antonio during the process of firing its city manager. That's when I wanted to call some of the council and say, "See, I told you so." But I wasn't the mayor anymore and so the "experts" in state law could do what they pleased without me.

In addition to the above, almost every meeting that year presented an occasion for me to be "front-stabbed" which is my term for the opposite of being back-stabbed, something that occurred after I left office. I'm not sure which is worse, but when such things occur, the way to keep your sanity and your spirit intact is to consider the source and remember that what you give you also get — eventually.

After our council meetings people — often people I didn't know — would hug me and ask how I can keep my cool in such circumstances. One councilmember who was especially nasty got a letter from a citizen who said that the councilmember's rudeness and bad behavior was unbecoming to the council and that the councilmember didn't have to like me but had to respect the office. This letter reflected what people said to me after our council meetings and when I met them at places like the supermarket or at city events. People encouraged me to "hang in there" and I received letters and note cards telling me that I had done a good job and that people were appalled at the behavior of some of the councilmembers.

The lesson I learned during my last year as mayor is that even at the worst of times, when you are feeling discouraged and ready to chuck it all, you may have support from people you never knew were on your side. I considered resigning from office but knowing that I had public support helped me to serve out my term. However, although I was encouraged by family, friends, local citizens, and my colleagues from other cities to run and hang in until the opposition would be out of office, I chose not to seek reelection. Life is too short to bang your head against a brick wall on purpose and after ten years in office I was due for some personal time. The rewarding thing was that although I thought that I had lost when the GOBS won, in reality I had won the respect and affection of the people who really mattered and so I really won and it was a humbling experience to receive accolades from my supporters. There are not enough superlatives in the English language to describe how good it feels to win with the people who really matter.

Although it didn't occur to me at the time, it's possible that if I had chosen to run for reelection, some people might have given me what folks refer to as the "pity vote." The pity vote can go to candidates who voters think deserve a reward for their fortitude in times of stress. It can also go to candidates who have run so many times and lost that folks vote for them out of pity. Sometimes that pity is misplaced; it should be transferred to city staff and the others on the council or board.

In my city, it's traditional for the mayor to announce whether or not he or she will run again during the announcements segment of a council meeting early enough before the election so that others may consider seeking the office. My announcement came from the heart and included things I felt needed to be said. Letters and comments I received afterward confirmed that some things "needed to be said."

My speech announcing that I would not seek reelection is in the last chapter of this book. It was carried in its entirety by one local newspaper and was misquoted by another, which seemed like a farewell misquote to me since that paper had misquoted me so often it became something that I expected.

When I chose not to run, I believed that the city would be in good hands after I left office because I was assured by two very capable and experienced people that they would run if I didn't. But as I should have expected (but ever optimistically did not even consider) politics took one of its strange twists. After I announced that I would not seek reelection, neither of those two people filed to run. Two people who had never served on council ran for mayor. So as I was leaving office, I was still learning about politics — that people don't always do what they say they will do — a lesson an optimist tries very hard not to learn no matter how many times it is taught.

My personal belief is that a person should serve on a council before attempting to be mayor. The mayor's duties are more complex and more numerous than most people think and having council experience helps you to better understand what needs to be done and how. During my times in office, I was very active in the Texas Municipal League, the Greater Bexar County Council of Cities and the Alamo Area Council of Governments. My observation in meeting various public officials was that more likely than not, someone who becomes mayor without any experience will have problems with staff, other councilmembers, citizens, citizens' groups, or just certain city situations, and generally serves only one term. It's not a job you can learn in a day, or even a year. Even the councilmembers who take advantage of the training offered by AACOG and TML say that it takes a year to feel reasonably comfortable and competent, another year to get really knowledgeable and to be able to be proactive in an effective way, and then it's time for election again in most cities.

And here is another truism: Most people in politics say that they love government and governance but genuinely dislike election time and campaigning. When you campaign at the small city, local levels you don't have a specialized staff or enough money to hire someone to do all the nitty-gritty things required in a campaign like mail-outs, press releases, and so forth. You must do these things yourself or have a trusted volunteer friend to help you. And while meeting and greeting the public can be fun for many candidates, dealing with opposing candidates, many of whom have no understanding of the issues but have vehement opinions on how things should be run and done, is a real challenge. It takes a major effort not to get totally defensive about your record and even a greater effort not to take criticism too personally. You have to learn to consider the source of the criticism, then cover-up your bruised ego and carry on. And you also have to learn to admit that some of the criticism may be valid!

When all is said, re-said, and said again, I will always think that holding political office is the absolute acme of volunteer service and the most challenging, exciting, and rewarding experience I have ever had, other than the rearing of my five children.

Chapter 7:

Women in Public Office

I have always loved this saying but I have no idea who said it: "Texas — where men are men and women hold public office."

Texas Governor Miriam A. ("Ma") Ferguson, was one of the first women governors in the United States. The wife of Governor James E. Ferguson who served from 1915 to 1917 and who was impeached, Ma served from 1925 to 1927 and again from 1933 to 1934. The story goes that since Jim Ferguson's impeachment prevented him from running for office in the 1924 election, he put his wife, Miriam, on the ballot. According to the *Texas Almanac* for 2004-2005, it was no secret that Jim Ferguson would influence his wife's administration, and their campaign slogan was, "Two governors for the price of one." Miriam won easily because, according to the *Almanac*, voters preferred "Fergusonism" to the Ku Klux Klan, which was becoming very powerful at that time.

We certainly have good examples of women officials who ran for office without being spouses of previously elected officials. Texas Governor Ann Richards served from 1991 to 1995, and San Antonio Mayor Lila Cockrell served as councilwoman from 1963-70 and 1973-

75, and was mayor from 1976 to 1981. Richards was the first Texas woman governor to win office in her own right and Cockrell was the first and only woman mayor of San Antonio and the first woman mayor of a major American city.

My favorite "why there should be more women in government" story has to do with our city's park restroom facility. (Somehow, in city government, the focus is so very often on drainage, garbage, potholes, and sewage in some form or other!) Leon Valley's park had only one restroom; it was convenient to the children's playground and family picnic areas. However, it was a significant distance from the area in which a local Little League played. People wanted a second restroom and, to immediately accommodate their requests, port-a-potties were installed at the opposite end of the park as a solution to the problem. Some park commissioners were concerned about the cost of a new properly-built restroom and considered the port-a-potties the final solution.

"Why can't they continue to use the port-a-potties?" one of the commissioners said, when I defended the need for a second restroom.

"Spoken like somebody who has never taken a little kid into port-a-potties," I replied. "They are afraid that they'll fall in and would rather wet themselves than go into port-a-potties."

"Well, then take them to the regular restroom," he said.

"Spoken like somebody who is not a mother," I explained. "Little kids don't tell you with enough time to walk that far to get there before the water falls."

The commissioner, always a reasonable man, thought for a moment, then said, "That's why we need more women in government. Men don't know these things."

He went on to comment on how the woman's viewpoint was important to issues that didn't involve restrooms and children's needs. I always liked that man and wished there were more like him! The restroom issue just confirmed what I had always known: Some men appreciate a woman's view and some don't. We need men like him in government as much as we need more women.

Almost every woman I have ever talked to about the women-in-government issue has had some problem with men who just can't bear to see women in positions of power, especially if that power is over men. Only a few say they never have had a problem but I wonder if they recognize it when it *is* a problem. Women my age (71 as this book is being written) don't always recognize when we are being "spoken down to" because we have grown accustomed to it, or at least accustomed to ignoring it.

I didn't realize how inured to such treatment I had become until I took a car care course with my daughter. As the male instructor spoke, my daughter was plainly agitated and told me that she would walk out if he continued to talk to us in "such a demeaning way." I hadn't noticed it but she had, and then I began to see what had angered her so much. At the break, she did another thing women my age (fiftyish at that time) would not usually do. She went up to the instructor and told him that he was very condescending and that he should not be talking down to us, because we were smarter than he thought. He looked startled and blushed, but the rest of his talk had a whole different tone. After that episode, I had a new respect for my daughter and the others in her generation. "Out of the mouths of babes " (or my babe) came emphasis on the idea that women want to be treated like women and not just babes!

Times have changed, thank heavens, and most of the time, at least on the surface, women do get the respect that they deserve. However, some pockets of resistance still remain and so my survey included the following questions:

- Have you experienced/observed any difference between women and men officeholders?
- If you are a woman, have you had problems with the Good Old Boys Society (GOBS) even now in the years after 2000?

What the Women Said in the Survey:

One former councilwoman said that back in the 1980s, she was only the third woman elected in her city. She never expected to encounter gender differences and could not remember having had any. She felt that the male councilmembers respected and supported her. She said that she never felt that she was a threat to them in any way and felt that they knew it.

Another woman said that she was not prepared to work closely with men because most of her volunteer work had been with groups composed mostly of women, who she says tend to listen, be responsive, and to respect others. Men, she observed, tend to want to control rather than converse, and to overpower the opposition. One of her male colleagues declared in a discussion that "consensus" was a dirty word and that he would never give up his own views. Based on her early experiences, she believed that there definitely are differences between women and men in public office. But, ever optimistic, she has noticed that younger men tend to listen and share opinions more easily than older ones. Also, that younger women are expressing their views more directly as they work with men more than did women of fifteen or twenty years ago.

One woman said that, although it's difficult to define how women's viewpoints differ from men's viewpoints, she believes that there are differences. One woman thought that men base their actions more strongly on concerns about what others, such as friends, etc., might think than women do. Another woman thought that there were many differences and that women were completely different in office, with one of those differences being that women are inclusive. One woman observed that men tend to be more ego-driven, while women are more caring, more willing to see the big picture, and more willing to compromise.

Among those who saw no difference among men and women in office was a woman who said that we all experience the same problems, same criticism and situations, and we all have to cope with these challenges. Another woman agreed, saying some are good and some are not, in either sex.

What Some Men Said in the Survey

Several men saw no difference between women and men in public office and, curiously, it appeared that the longer a man held office, the fewer differences he saw between women and men in public office.

One of the men agreed with one of the women respondents in that he said there was no difference between women and men in office; some members of each gender are excellent and some members of each gender do not perform well, he noted.

One man said that he didn't know if the differences among councilmembers are gender-related or simply differences in expertise, experiences, and interests in certain specific issues and/or specific areas of government. Another man agreed and noted that each councilmember had distinct viewpoints that were not related to gender.

Yet another man thought there was no difference but noted that his council had only one woman member on it in seven years. Another man's city has had women in office most of the time that he has been in office and he saw no gender differences.

One respondent said, regarding differences, that women are usually prettier than men and added that he knew it was sexist to say such a thing and he was sorry about that. His feeling, which he said was undocumented, was that men display more patience with the process of government than women do.

Another man believed women tend to be more intense. Yet another said that men seem more pragmatic, while women are more "quick to judge." One man thought that women seem to be more caring in their nature, but another said that women seem to be more aggressive on division where conflicts arise.

Still another man said that women in office are sometimes reluctant to use their talents and assert the authority of office. Another man concluded that there are obvious differences in approach and resolution of issues, but his experience has been that women can do it as well as men, and in some instances, better.

Women and the GOBS

About half of the women respondents had problems with the Good Old Boys Society and the other half did not.

Some women, who had run for office when they were the only women in that position, were supported by some members of the ruling GOBS of their cities as well as outsiders. One had problems with GOBS at first but says conditions have changed and continue to change. Others were fortunate in that the GOBS in their entities left office and became obscure.

One woman says that problems with GOBS have continued and that when she first announced that she would run, she was told that she "wasn't a big enough bitch."

One woman experienced no problems with her colleagues or the professional staff but noted some gender-related problems with certain special interest groups. Another had no problems with GOBS at the local level but observed some at the state level.

My experience with the GOBS is that if you are useful to them, that is to say that you can get enough votes to defeat someone they don't like, the GOBS will support you. But I would expect that this is not a gender issue — it's an election strategy issue. However, to keep the GOBS support, you have to follow the GOBS line and consider their wishes and opinions about issues before your own opinions or the opinions of anyone else. Again, I don't think this is really a gender problem. Men would get the same treatment in GOBS City.

Sometimes people say that women take criticism too personally but my observation is that this also is not necessarily a gender problem. And sometimes, from some people, the criticism gets personal. The trick is to consider the source of the criticism. It may come from someone who has a chip on the shoulder or from someone who is always against certain issues, and who gets personal because that's the only way that person knows how to operate. The way to survive in politics is to develop a thick skin which doesn't mean that you won't listen to criticism — it could be valid — but that you can take it without becoming devastated. You really can't please all of the people all of the time.

Sometimes I think that some women are so preoccupied with feelings — theirs and the feelings of others — that they forget to be results-oriented when making decisions and taking action. It's not that we should trample on others' feelings, but I think that in government where you use other people's money to accomplish goals that not all of the people care about, feelings have to take a lower priority than results. The question is not "How do I, we, or they feel about this," but "How will this action do the greatest good for the greatest number of people?" The longer I was in office, the more results-oriented I became. I did make an effort to continue membership in all — or mostly — female social and professional groups so that I would keep in touch with touchy-feely attitudes. I must admit that I often found myself wondering what all the fuss was about when members would be upset about hurting someone's feelings or having their own feelings hurt. I would go home and wonder if I could be losing my femininity. Every now and then someone tells me that I think like a man and I never know if it is a compliment or an insult. I do think that generally speaking, being results-oriented instead of feelings-oriented seems to be more a male than female trait and I'm sure that somebody could argue with me about that, but it is my observation. I also know that "generally speaking" can get a person in a lot of trouble.

I do know this for sure: I have been around long enough to know that no political rules are absolute, but when it comes to male-female relationships, there are some behavior patterns that predominate even if many people don't want to admit it. Again, these are not rules but only my observations.

For example, I've noticed that men whose mothers and/or wives have jobs outside the home and/or are community leaders, and men who have daughters in the workplace are more likely to treat women as equals. Men who have worked for a long time with women, either in paid jobs or as volunteers, also tend to treat women more as equals.

Younger men, and by younger I don't mean age in numbers but a matter of attitude, also tend to treat women as equals.

However, some men whose wives are full-time homemakers, who are the only breadwinners in the home, and/or whose wives treat them deferentially as rulers of the roost even at social functions, tend to treat other women as they would "the wife." And the term "other women" includes their colleagues in public office.

In all fairness to men, sometimes women in public office surrender their equality until they get confidence in their own ability to do the job, especially if they lack the background, experience, and confidence needed in a political career.

One reality about men in public service is that some men simply cannot accept a woman in a position of power. During my tenure as mayor, one of our male community leaders decided that he wanted to be on a certain board. He asked several staff members to ask me to appoint him but, true to form, just couldn't bring himself to ask me directly. From past experience, I knew that this individual usually took over any group that he happened to be in. He could dominate all discussions, oppose any idea that was not his, and eventually some folks would give up and leave, thus making space for people who supported his views to take their places. This board was exceptional and composed of people who worked together for the city and not just to promote themselves or their own personal projects and concepts, and the chairman was a woman. Needless to say, I did not even consider his appointment and that may have contributed to political repercussions and opposition in my last term as mayor. However, I don't regret my decision.

Sometimes, even in situations where women and men are working together in government committees, people who ought to know better will slip up and forget that some women have equal rank with the men in the room. When I represented the Greater Bexar County Council of Cities at a special taskforce meeting of elected officials, I was the only female elected official on the taskforce. The person taking the roll call properly referred to each man seated on the dais as "The Honorable Bill Smith, The Honorable John Jones, The Honorable . . . (whomever)", and when it came to my name he hesitated for a few seconds and finally said, "Ummm . . . and . . . Marcy Meffert." It brought down the house when I said, "Here, and just for the record, I'm just as 'Honorable' as the rest of these guys."

Some Hints for Women in the Public Eye

Women do have some handicaps just because they are women.

For example, traditionally in this country, women don't greet people with handshaking as much as men do, but in politics everybody shakes hands. Handshaking in political life is an interesting custom, especially if you consider the origin of the practice. The origin of the handshake, I've read, is to show the person you have just met that you are not concealing a weapon.

For some women, shaking hands is a new experience. You soon learn that after you wash your hands in the restroom, you need to dry your hands with a couple of towels so that you don't present a wet hand to shake with somebody you meet right outside the restroom door.

Women's purses are a liability in a handshake society. They fall off your shoulder and make you look awkward as you try to hold them up, but if you put them somewhere, such as on your chair at the luncheon table or in a corner behind a drape, you wonder if your purse will be there when you return. (I'm not implying that your colleagues will steal your purse but not all in the room are colleagues!) I learned that when going to an event at which I will be working a room, the practical answer is to put my drivers' license, a credit card, and some cash in a coin purse that fits into my jacket pocket and I leave my purse at home. The coin purse goes in one pocket with a handkerchief or tissue, and your business cards go in the other pocket. Save plastic name-tag holders to serve as containers for business cards: remove the pins, insert the cards, and they will stay clean and neat in your pocket, purse, or briefcase.

Women's clothing can be a handicap and can give new meaning to the phrase "being in the public eye." For example, women in public office have to give up wearing things like short skirts and sundresses to public events. The reality is that if some man is looking at your thighs or cleavage, he is not likely to be listening to what you are saying. Business attire creates business attitudes.

Also, when you are invited to speak or just sit on a dais, especially if it is on a raised stage, you need to wear either a long skirt or pants. Your knees, while attractive to the man in your life, are not a businesslike sight when framed by your slip and skirt and viewed from the audience. Sitting with your knees together in the finishing-school pose gets old and crampy sooner than anyone thinks.

If you are in a huggy group, you need to learn how to hug without getting lipstick on a man's shirt collar or a woman's shoulder. When you are a short woman, you find yourself bumping your nose on tall men's tie tacks and belt buckles but that's not a problem exclusive to political life. As a short person, I need to have my eyeglasses adjusted regularly from hugs that bend them. I'd still rather be hugged though!

Some years ago, I had a big bear hug from a colleague just before I was to give a luncheon speech at an affair honoring certain women in the community. The hug broke the temple off my glasses, and since I can't read without glasses, I wore my slightly askew spectacles anyway — one carries on as expected. The previous speaker, always a women's advocate, said that he was glad to see women getting a "bigger piece of the pie" in community honors. With my glasses askew, I responded with one of my favorite lines, one that seemed to bring down the house, which was: "We women deserve to get a bigger piece of the pie. After all, we helped to bake the damn thing."

While broken glasses don't detract from a good line or an inspiring speech, often high-pitched or "girly" women's voices can detract and distract people from speakers' messages. Another distraction/detraction is using a girly voice and ending each sentence in the tone of a question; it sounds cloying, weak, and indecisive. I think it is possible for a woman to lower the pitch of her voice so that she sounds more convincing and confident; it takes practice and is worth doing. I once attended a council meeting in which a new female mayor greeted each person who came to the podium as if we were in her living room, with a girly-voiced "Hello, how are you, glad you could be with us today." The intent was to make people feel welcome but it tended to unnerve them when they were presenting something as serious as a request for zoning changes or permits. The newbie mayor eventually learned to be more businesslike at meetings.

Women and the Men Who Support us

In the past in politics, women worked on campaigns for male candidates by stuffing envelopes, baking cookies, and making sandwiches for campaign parties, going door-to-door to get votes, and, when married to a candidate, being surrogate candidates, single parents, and in general, all around good worker-helpers. Just as male candidates were helped (or hindered) by their spouses and campaign workers, women need help and support from their husbands and male campaigners.

My husband, a dentist, has attained international prominence in his profession, and for many years I teased him about his "groupies" — former students and people who attended his lectures given throughout the world who would gather around him to ask questions. Wherever we went — hotel lobbies, parties, in restaurants, and so forth, I would smile and wait patiently while we became late for meeting friends and while dinners cooled as fast as my interest in teeth. I spent many evenings listening to his colleagues talk about professional matters and learned that if I uttered a few buzz words about his specialties of periodontics and dental implants, people thought I actually knew what they were talking about. Then they could comfortably continue their conversations with him without having to make small talk with me. I believed that it was my job as "the wife" to support him in his work.

After I became a mayor he tried to play the same role for me. Fortunately, he does not have a macho-type ego, so he was able to maintain a sense of humor about being a spousal unit instead of the main man. For example, when he would be following me around at an event, wearing his name tag that said, "Hello, I'm Rollie Meffert." People would greet me first, then look at his name tag and say, "And so, Mr. Meffert, what is it that you do?"

One year, he joined me at a breakfast meeting of the Texas Municipal League where a group of other mayors and I were discussing upcoming resolutions for legislation that would be presented to us at a meeting after the breakfast. The conversation centered on the reasons we planned to support or not support some of the resolutions. After about twenty minutes, my husband leaned over and whispered in my ear, "I have no idea what these people are talking about." And I whispered back, "And how does that feel?"

Fortunately, by the time I went into politics our children were grown and gone, and so organizing mealtime for a family was no longer a priority, nor was it as expensive for two adults to eat out often as it would have been if our five children were still home. When I was doing the mayor job at luncheon or dinner meetings, my husband learned to cook frozen dinners in the microwave. He would ask, "Is this a black plate night for me?" (Most come on black plates.) So when the garden club needed saucers for a dish garden project at our local nursing home, I said I had plenty and brought 47 of them, explaining to the ladies that when you hold public office, your husband collects a lot of black plates.

We've laughed about his role as the mayor's husband many times and I tell these stories to emphasize how women need spousal support to hold public office as much as men do and how grateful I was to have that support from my husband. He often said that he owed me for all the times I supported him and, ever honest, I agreed, "Yes, you do."

Male city managers are among the other men in women's political life. No chapter on women in politics would be complete without this tale about a female mayor and a rather macho city manager. Early in my first term as mayor, at a state meeting I met another female mayor who had her arm in a cast.

"How did that happen?" I asked, making conversation.

"City manager broke my arm," she replied.

That certainly got the mouth-dropping attention of everyone seated at our table.

Then she related how she and the city manager were in disagreement about what another individual had said about an issue. She told the city manager that she would call the person, get him to repeat what he said, and then they could stop discussing it. She reached for the phone; the city manager grabbed the phone away from her and in the process, broke her forearm when he slammed down the receiver.

"So what did you do about that," I asked, stunned that such a thing would happen.

"He's history," she replied. "He's fired."

So I returned to city hall and told the tale of woe to our city manager and added that I hoped we would never come to blows and broken arms. And we never did.

I was fortunate that most male councilmembers who served with me knew how to deal with female colleagues. Also, our city had several female department heads and so staff also functioned without "the woman thing," as many of us call the macho attitude.

As noted previously in this chapter, one of the things that has always perplexed me is that I have often been told that I "think like a man." The mystery to me is that I'm never sure if that statement is meant to be a compliment or an insult. I choose to take it as a compliment because it is useful in politics to be able to think like your colleagues and/or your opponents, regardless of their gender or your own!

I grew up in a Polish matriarchy in which women were equals and could speak their minds. I never learned to manipulate male colleagues by fluttering my eyelashes and sweet-talking them into doing my bidding. I would feel silly, and to me silly does not get the respect which is vital to success in public office. It's nice if people like you, but it is more important for people to respect you and, I should add, mutual respect has to be the rule if women and men are to work together to accomplish good things in government.

Chapter 8:

It Can Be Fun!

In between the challenges, wins and losses, frustrations and disappointments, holding political office can be just plain fun, and so I asked my colleagues, "What part of holding office is fun?"

Just having a title before your name can be fun, many agreed. Although some officeholders get embarrassed by the attention we get when we are in public, I think most of us enjoy the spotlight, even if it's not a mega-spotlight. It's nice to be recognized during the VIP introductions at various public events; it's good to get a reserved parking place every now and then; it's great to get recognition from your peers at political conventions and meetings; and having a title before your name has a delightful sound, whether or not you admit it even to yourself — and several survey respondents admitted it.

One female councilmember noted that after years of being someone's wife and someone's mother, which were titles she was pleased to have, it was very nice to be the main person at times and to hear her husband referred to as "Councilmember Susan's husband." Surely many female officials can relate to this; I know I can.

I recall an event in which we were organizing neighborhood

groups to promote recycling and a person came up to me and asked, "Are you the mayor's wife?"

"No," I replied, feeling oh-so-good about it, "I'm the mayor. Can I help you?"

Then there was the time I was working with Boy Scouts to clean up debris after one of our city's floods. I sternly lectured the boys on how they must wear the gloves they had been given, and they must carefully wash their hands after the clean up and before they ate anything, due to the unknowns in the debris. Having had five children, I repeated the instructions three times, and then asked again, "Do you boys understand?"

One of the boys listened as little boys do, and then finally asked, "I hear all this but when is that mayor going to show up?"

The troop leaders pointed to me and said, "This is the mayor." I guess I sounded more motherly than mayoral to the boys.

Riding in festival parades was fun when mothers would point to me and tell their daughters, "Look at the lady mayor." Speaking at career days at local elementary schools was fun for the same reason. I still treasure the thank-you note I received from a third grader who said, "Now that I know a lady can be mayor, I want to be one when I grow up."

But you don't have to be a *female* official to enjoy the celebrity and having the title of mayor, councilman, judge, commissioner, etc. One mayor, male, said, in the survey form, it was fun "watching unsuspecting people's faces when you tell them that you are the mayor."

Any interaction with kids is fun. School board trustees listed attending school events when kids perform at the top of the list of fun things in office. They also enjoyed events that featured recognition awards and going to schools where they read to kids. As mayor, I enjoyed handing out plaques and certificates that celebrated anyone's achievements, whether they were adults or children.

One of our city's councilmembers, Marilyn Bellows, taught "American Culture" to Chinese students at the University of Texas at San Antonio. Each semester she would bring her students to tour our city hall, talk to the mayor, visit various departments, and speak with department heads. It was fun to explain our city government to foreign students, especially those from a country which is experiencing democracy as a relatively new concept. As usual, they were amazed that our city didn't pay a salary to the elected officials and amazed at the amount of time that anyone would spend on a job that paid no salary. Bellows would explain that Americans have a tradition of volunteerism, and the students' expressions would be one of surprise. I have lived in other countries and it has always appeared to me that Americans do more volunteer work than others. Once a Chinese student asked if a state or federal official had to approve the voters' choices in our elections, which was a question I'd never thought of in our society. The Chinese students were always pleased to know that I had visited their country and their eyebrows would always go up when they heard that my visit was during the 1995 Fourth World Conference on Women. They were familiar with the controversies and issues surrounding the Conference and would laugh when I said that neither I nor my friends were parading around China in the nude. (Chinese officials spread that rumor and it was said that there were groups of Chinese cops waiting in areas with blankets to cover the shameless foreign hussies' nudity.)

The subject of volunteerism in America was primary when a group of Muslim women from several Middle Eastern countries visited our city as part of their tour of the area. Some were veiled and some were not. All were educated women leaders in their countries and they were asking Americans who worked with volunteers how they too could get such action in their homelands. One said, "What do you do, work your volunteers to death?" I said that nobody had died from volunteering in our city, but some of them went on to use their experiences and contacts to run for political office and to some people that is a fate worse than death.

Just as one person's trash is another person's treasure, one person's fun is another torture. Not everyone likes to be social every day of the week with anyone who comes to visit, but it does go with the political territory. I learned early on that socializing and networking is how you get the wheels of government to turn for your own benefit and that of your city. The truth, as it appears to me, is that when you need to get something done and you need the support of other political entities to get that thing done, it's not who or what you know; it's who knows you. It's who you can call on the phone and say, "Hi, this is Mayor XYZ, remember when we met at the ABC luncheon? Well, I have a problem that I think and hope you can help me solve . . ."

To me, interacting and working with city, county, and school district staff is part of the fun when you are the elected official. Most public officials emphasized how much they enjoyed the personal inter-actions with individuals and with citizens groups, with professional staff, speaking to various civic groups, meeting and socializing with people from all walks of life and from other cities and states. While socializing was considered fun, almost nobody said that campaigning was fun, and in fact campaigning headed the list of things that were the "worst part of holding or running for office."

One former mayor said that having citizens and city employees drop by to visit in the mayor's office and to spend time exchanging ideas was fun. Annual barbecues for city employees, retired officials and their families in the city park were the best of times for one former official.

Sometimes work is fun. Several respondents noted that working with groups to get goals accomplished was fun. They listed as "fun" accomplishing the goals of the majority of people, accomplishing positive improvements — especially those that improved the quality of life — and finding the funding for those improvements.

One mayor said that it's fun to "preside at council meetings when city council members and citizens are working together to reach a resolution of tough problems," and another said that it's fun "to help people work out their problems through a government system that is confounding to them."

Fun to one official was "seeing the city grow and knowing I had a hand in it." Another said "being the example of change and what good government is all about" is fun. Yet another said that seeing citizens getting involved was fun. Several said that attending Texas Municipal League meetings was fun because one can network and interact with "the best elected officials in the state."

While "just being part of all that is going on in the city," "making a difference," and "the feeling that you are helping the community with your decisions" is fun, it's even more fun to get thanks and appreciation from citizens for a good job done, said several officials.

Sometimes, a council meeting can be fun and silly. I recall a presentation of a zoning case on an overhead projector that begged for humor. As the development department's director was presenting the case, from somewhere inside the projector a cockroach appeared and proceeded to crawl up and down the streets of the proposed subdivision. It also crawled up and down Bandera Road, perhaps to find a snack among our many fast-food restaurants? Then it trampled across our park and library, strolled along our Huebner Creek bed, and finally rested atop city hall like a scene from *Roachzilla Conquers Leon Valley*. It was embarrassing but our development director, ever poised, continued to talk, trying to ignore it. However, I could see that everyone was fascinated by the roach's stroll through Leon Valley being projected upon a screen. So I felt I just had to say, "I can see that we don't have all the bugs out of this project yet." It sure broke up the meeting and perhaps the laughter scared the cockroach because it disappeared from the screen, presumably back to the inside of the projector, never to return.

Sometimes what's fun for others in your city is not fun for you. Our city had an annual July 4th celebration that involved a parade and various games for adults and children afterward in our park and community area. In its early years, a pie-eating contest was held with various officials and citizens as eaters. I was asked to be in the first wave of pie-eaters, and when I declined some folks thought that I was too prissy or ladylike to put my face in a pie. I didn't want to say anything that would spoil their fun, but I actually have a strong moral objection to all eating contests. With so many people starving in this world, it seems obscene to me to waste food in such a gross manner. I begged off participating in the contest as tactfully as I could and then the next time I saw the committee, I explained my position: I don't object to other people enjoying eating contests but I just can't bring myself to participate, on moral grounds. I was grateful that people respected my position. Nobody asked me again and eventually the eating contests were abandoned. I hope I didn't spoil anyone's fun, but even when you are in politics, in relatively insignificant matters (to others), you have to follow your conscience.

One of the great joys of being the mayor is that you get invited to all sorts of ceremonies and events as a representative of the city. After a few events, I learned how important it was to bring along a proclamation of thanks or congratulations for whoever was being honored or whatever was being celebrated. Bringing proclamations to events is not listed in the duties of the mayor in the how-to manuals but it is a very important thing to remember!

I was invited to several Eagle Scout awards events each year and completely enjoyed them. It is so gratifying to see young people accomplishing their goals while doing community service. As a parent of five children and former Girl Scout leader, I understood how the Scouts' parents and leaders felt to see the children achieve the ultimate in Scouting. I found my eyes tearing up as if the children were mine during the ceremonies. Many were held in churches and so I learned a lot about the customs of other religions, too.

After I mentioned to the pastor of our local Lutheran church that I had attended a jazz mass in New York, he invited me to a jazz mass at his church which was being held to honor the retiring bishop of the area. What fun it was to hear the music, and what fun the after-mass potluck dinner was! The bishop had a marvelous sense of humor and we traded wisecracks well enough to have several parishioners suggest that we go on the road with "the bishop and mayor show." I shall never forget the jokes about "Lutheran food" made by the pastor and others when they discovered that I, too, was a fan of Garrison Keillor and "A Prairie Home Companion" broadcasts on National Public Radio. In fact I shall not forget any of the services I attended at the Lutheran church. I guess that I should point out that I was raised Roman Catholic, and when I was growing up, pre-Vatican II, I could not have attended services in a non-Catholic church.

As mayor, I frequently attended services and events in Mormon, Baptist, Catholic, Lutheran, and other churches. Many times it was to attend funeral services — not really in the category of "fun" but events which give you a feeling of doing something worthwhile and significant to others. A couple of weeks after I was elected, I attended the first funeral as mayor/representative of the city. It was for a person who had been one of our city's leaders. I walked into the visitation room to pay my respects to the widow and her family, and as I approached the casket I heard people whispering, "It's the mayor . . . the mayor's here . . ." I went to the visitation because I thought it was the right thing to do to honor a former city volunteer, but I did not anticipate that the mayor's being there would be so significant to the family.

It may sound strange, but the visitation was my first realization that I was a public figure, even if it was as a VIP in a small city, and I was somewhat in awe of the whole concept and the responsibilities attached to being a public figure. I found it to be humbling and an almost overwhelming experience that anyone would find my presence anywhere to be so important! I knew that being the mayor was more prestigious than being a councilmember, and councilmembers were noticed more than ordinary citizens, but the whole public official aura just hadn't sunk into my brain until that day.

Finally, to me it has been fun to attend events since I left office and have people come up and tell me what a great job I did and that I am missed. We all need an ego stroke like that after we leave a job. I wrote a weekly column for local weekly newspapers called "What's Up in Leon Valley", and a year later people are still telling me that they miss the column. How good can life get? I always joked that only fifty people read the column but it would appear that the column was read more than I thought. Sometimes you are being more effective than you think you are . . . which is, of course, something to remember when times are tough.

Representing Your City Outside of the City

Like many of my colleagues, I enjoyed going to meetings with the Texas Municipal League. The seminars, workshops, and other programs always provided insight and new ideas on how to do things better. Interaction with other public officials was a bonus since you could find out what worked or didn't work in other cities.

Breakfasts for cities of various populations were among the featured events of TML state meetings. Since our city's population was about 10,000, one day I would attend the breakfast for cities with populations of 10,000 or less, and then the next day I would go to the breakfast for cities with populations of 10,000 to 25,000. The main thing that I learned at the breakfasts was that the basic problems of smaller and larger cities (maintenance of police, fire protection, street programs, sewer/water services, and prevention of flooding, enforcing code violations, etc.) are often the same or similar, and listening to the officials of any size city I learned about their solutions to problems and got new ideas for our city.

As a councilmember, I volunteered to serve on various TML boards and committees. One of these was the Small Cities Advisory Council which provided TML with input on the needs of small cities. One of the first issues discussed at a SCAC meeting was whether or not small cities would object to placing the actual names of various travelers' facilities (restaurants, fuel, motels) before their cities' freeway exit signs. At that time, only the generic symbols, such as a gas pump or knife and fork, were shown on signs. A bill was introduced to allow trade names like McDonald's, Texaco, and Motel 6 to be included with the symbols. We all agreed it was a good idea. From a mother's viewpoint, I surely would want to know if the restaurant was McDonald's where my children could be comfortable and have a play area or a nicer "adult restaurant," and I certainly wanted a family-friendly hotel/motel when on the road with five children, and all of the council members agreed with me. Others on the SCAC thought knowing which gas company was at an exit would be a benefit to folks who wanted to use a specific gas credit card. The bill passed in the Legislature and now every time I drive down a highway and see one of the brand name signs, I smile and think, "I had a piece of that idea and it is really a good one!"

I also represented our city at the Greater Bexar County Council of Cities where mayors and city managers met to discuss various issues that we all shared. It, too, was a learning situation and an opportunity to meet some very dedicated people. Mayors have a special bond, and getting sympathy from people who can understand why you need sympathy is a truly rewarding and stress-busting experience.

However, when you are the new kid on the block, interacting with other more experienced public officials and officials with higher ranks than yours can be intimidating. Many of the mayors had been in office longer than I but eventually, after several elections, I became one of the old-timers and I suppose one of those who seemed more knowledgeable than the newbies.

Among the jobs for which I volunteered was to represent the GBCCC on the AACOG board of directors and I eventually chaired that organization for two terms. My first meetings were definitely intimidating. The board consisted of county judges, county commissioners, state representatives and senators, and others — all of whom, I was certain, were vastly more knowledgeable than I would ever be. Equally awesome was the fact that we voted on funding for many projects where the cost figures had mind-boggling (to me) numbers of zeros after the dollar signs. As one who suffers from trepidation at writing checks of $100 or more, voting to spend taxpayer monies at the six or more zero level was downright scary. But with the encouragement and mentoring of a couple of longtime board members, and the assistance of the very professional AACOG staff, I did my best to read all the material and learn as fast as I could.

During my first year on the AACOG board, a resolution was requested by a senior citizen group in which the board was to censure/protest a TV commercial because the senior group said the commercial was derogatory — that it made seniors look helpless and inept. In the commercial, an elderly lady has a house fire; firefighters come and attempt to put out the fire, but they leave before it is totally out. The elderly lady is left alone amidst the mess, and she continues to try to smash out the fire with a broom.

When I got my packet with the resolution to protest the ad, I went to the president of our area's senior group and asked her what she thought. She said she thought everybody should "just lighten up," and that protesting the commercial was silly. I also thought that if anyone should protest, it should be the firefighters' union since they looked really bad, leaving the woman alone with the house still burning, and also that the old lady looked pretty tough since she didn't give up — she appeared anything but helpless and inept.

During the discussion, I told the board what our senior group president said and what I thought about the commercial, and also I didn't think it was appropriate for the board to be passing resolutions about TV commercials anyway. As I was speaking, I saw the judges, commissioners, mayors, and others nodding their heads in agreement and I had one of those glorious moments known only to those who have had them. I thought, "Hot damn, I just became a member of the club!" The board did not pass the resolution and the commercial went off the air because it was just plain dumb.

Sometimes you have to decline certain kinds of fun not for moral reasons but because you are too clueless and/or skill-less to join in. Each year, AACOG sponsors a Pony Express celebration to kickoff, or more appropriately to ride-into the holiday season. Officials and others ride their horses from town to town in the 12-county AACOG region and end up with a festive ceremony at Fort Sam Houston in San Antonio. Asked if I would like to ride to the ceremony on horseback with the other riders, I had to decline the honor even when promised that I would get a very tame critter. My reason was that I grew up in the inner city and the only large animal that I'd ever experienced was a football player I dated in high school. I am willing to try almost anything at least once, but I don't do horses!

Having been a humor writer in my other life, I found that I still enjoyed getting laughs when I spoke at events or was the emcee/chairman of various meetings, and once people knew I was interested they sent me many very funny emails with material to use when speaking in public. I'm including two of them in this chapter so that others can use them when they are presiding.

Most of the people in politics I've met can laugh at each other and themselves. The following came to me in an email which said these are actual quotes from actual Texas politicos. I have purposely left the names out to protect the guilty:

- "It just makes good sense to put all your eggs in one basket," said a Texas state representative who was speaking on an amendment requiring all revenues to go into the state treasury.
- "Ain't nothin' in the middle of the road but yellow stripes and dead armadillos," said a Texas agricultural commissioner.
- "And now, will y'all stand and be recognized?" said a Texas house speaker to a group of handicapped people in wheelchairs.
- "Dallas salutes a person who can buy a piece of art but not a person who can create one." Anonymous.
- "No thanks, once was enough," said a Texas governor when asked if he had been born again.
- "Oh good. Now he'll be bi-ignorant," said a Texas commissioner when told that a Texas governor was studying Spanish.
- "I'd just make a little bit of money, I wouldn't make a whole lot," said a Texas house speaker defending himself against the charge that he would personally profit from a bill he introduced.
- "Well, there never was a Bible in the room," said a Texas governor when asked about repeatedly lying about a situation.
- "If ignorance ever goes to $40 a barrel, I want drillin' rights on that man's head," said a Texas commissioner about a president's policies.
- "If it's dangerous to talk to yourself, it's probably even dicier to listen," said a Texas commissioner.

- "I move we recess to go outside and throw up," said a Texas house speaker during a budget hearing.
- "Let's do this in one foul sweep," said a Texas house speaker.
- "I want to thank each and every one of you for having extinguished yourselves this session," said a Texas house speaker.
- "We'll run it up the flagpole and see who salutes that booger," said the same Texas house speaker.
- "There's a lot of uncertainty that's not clear in my mind," said a Texas house speaker.
- "I can explain it for you but I can't understand it for you." Anonymous.
- "There are still places where people think that the function of the media is to provide information." Anonymous.

Someone sent me an email of Texas "Figgers of Speech" and their meanings that would certainly be communication aids to Texas transplanted folks . . . the ones who say, "I wasn't born in Texas but I got here as fast as I could." Here is some Texas talk:

- As welcome as a skunk at a lawn party. (Self-explanatory)
- Tighter than bark on a tree. (Not very generous)
- Big hat, no cattle. (All talk and no action)
- We've howdied but we ain't shook yet. (We've made a brief acquaintance, but have not been formally introduced)
- He thinks the sun came up just to hear him crow. (He has a pretty high opinion of himself)
- It's so dry the trees are bribin' the dogs. (We really need a little rain around here)
- Just because a chicken has wings doesn't mean it can fly. (Appearances can be deceptive)
- This ain't my first rodeo. (I've been around awhile)
- He looks like the dog's been keepin' him under the porch. (Not the most handsome of men)

- They ate supper before they said grace. (Living in sin)
- Time to paint your butt white and run with the antelope. (Stop arguing and do as you're told)
- As full of wind as a corn-eating horse. (Rather prone to boasting)
- You can put your boots in the oven but that doesn't make them biscuits. (You can say whatever you want about something, but it doesn't change what it is)

And the saying that I would wish for anyone running for or holding public office:

- We're pickin' in tall cotton. (Things are going well)

Different Definitions of Fun

Interaction with people can be a different kind of fun when you associate with those whose lives are fascinating and inspirational. I feel privileged to have met people whose lives are almost heroic and who should get medals of honor and valor for surviving their daily lives. I have been privileged to work with volunteers who gladly give their time and energies to make good things happen for others. The loyalty and friendship of our city staff was a special joy to me. Few things can raise your spirits more than when a city employee who has had numerous job offers says, "I will stay here as long as you do." Or when a city employee tells you that you are doing a good job and makes extra efforts to help you do your job well.

It was fun to be with my favorite mentor and our city's Mayor Emeritus Ken Alley and his wife, Esther. Ken, even after he passed age 90, still had a fire in his heart for the city he helped found and I recall a council meeting when a person who was a constant critic of the city spoke during a Citizens to be Heard meeting protesting a council action. Ken got up and minced no words telling the protestor how he felt about people who come to council only to complain, never want to be part of the solution, and just want to criticize — and it was very clear that Ken didn't feel good about such people. Sadly, Ken lost his battle with age and cancer at 94 and the whole city mourned his passing. I wrote a poem about Ken, as I often do when I need therapy, in this case, grief therapy.

THE FIRE WITHIN
(Written for Ken Alley, who kept the fire within and inspired others to do the same.)

Each of us has a fire within us.
Sometimes it's merely a spark,
Sometimes it's an eager ember
Waiting to burst into flame.

For some of us, causes are the fuel
For some of us, issues fan the flame
And the flame ignites a torch
That leads others out of darkness.

Some of us let the sparks go out,
        Allow embers to die for lack of tinder.
The fire within remains unlit
So some neither lead nor follow.

But for those who find the fuel and fan the flames
And for those who carry the torch or follow it,
The fire within lights the way
To brighter days for all of us.

                                by Marcy Meffert

I had profound admiration for many other senior citizens in our city who took care of each other and remained active and interested in the community regardless of age. One couple, Ethel and Ray Mason, who were in their eighties, were amazing to me. Ethel would take Ray to council meetings, city events, and meetings and sling his wheelchair out of the trunk of their car, unfold it, help him to sit in it, and wheel him up ramps and through hallways so both of them could express their opinions at council or just enjoy social events.

And then there were Frank Zavala, Brian Hough, and George and Norma Parr who always helped with the Xeriscape Program. Norma's health was not always good but she would do what she could to find yards for the judging and to volunteer George as a driver for the judges if she was not up to it. Frank chaired the judging of the yards after I became mayor and couldn't chair it anymore. Brian continued to work with the program even after he moved out of the city. He worked with Dee Emory of Gardening Volunteers of South Texas who gave us the Master Gardeners' support from the very beginning when we were not sure how the program would work. I learned early on that forming partnerships with people and groups who had expertise that you did not have was the key to making a project successful. We could not have had a Xeriscape Program without the help of the Master Gardeners.

Our Los Leones Student Arts Festival became a success due to the early loyal volunteer efforts of Frank and Lettie Zavala and Lucy and Henry Garcia. Frank and Henry were still involved with the project in its tenth year. They would come early and stay until the very end and cheerfully do whatever needed doing. Later, two very busy working moms chaired the event for three years each — M'lissa Chumbley and

Susan Hillje. Susan's husband, Ken, was volunteered too. Katie Gwaltney and Gail Tribble spent many hours organizing the judging of student art works. Katie also pulled together a super fiftieth city anniversary celebration on short notice. Staff and teachers in the Northside School District and board members of the Northside Education Foundation also were vital to the success of Los Leones. I received a Time Warner Home Town Hero award as the founder/chairman of Los Leones but the real heroes were the committee volunteers, the staff of the city and school district, and the two chairs, Chumbley and Hillje, who presided over its rapid growth into a real festival event.

I will always be grateful to all the members of the Leon Valley Civic Affairs Committee who supported the arts festival and worked on the committee's other events. Their efforts were the reasons all of our city's social events were so successful. Social events in a city are the glue that binds people together whether they work on the sponsoring committees or just attending functions. A community is made up of people more than it is merely buildings, streets, and concrete, and when people work together for the common good everyone feels ownership in the city. Encouraging that ownership is the real fun of holding office as many of my colleagues said and as I experienced.

I can't possibly name all of the 104 volunteers who served our city while I was mayor but each one inspired me more than they probably realized. Nobody ever accomplishes anything totally by his or her own efforts and I was fortunate to have help from people who, although they had other obligations, responded when I asked and did a super job to make our community better. I was also fortunate to have the support of professional and loyal city staff. If ever there is a definition of "fun," it's working with such people.

If you are lucky, the fun doesn't end when you retire from office. Sometimes you become an elder statesman character even if you don't think of yourself in that context. People ask your opinion on city issues even when your opinion no longer matters in any official capacity. I have been asked to serve on various boards and committees as a citizen and I must say that it is fun to work with old friends and colleagues without the responsibility of being the one upon whose desk the buck stops.

Finally, after you leave office it's fun to look over your press clippings, enjoy your successes, lament your failures, and remember the people with whom you shared this most exciting, interesting phase of your life.

Chapter 9

Sitcom Characters and the Meeting from Government Hell

Several years ago, a group of experienced officeholders and staff from the Texas Municipal League put on a skit at one of the state meetings that was a how-not-to-do example for public officials. The scene was a city council meeting but it could very well be a school board or any other governmental meeting. The characters in the skit violated every rule of decorum and all of *Robert's Rules of Order*. Since seeing the skit, I've often imagined writing a sitcom set in a small city that had characters you wouldn't want to meet in public life. The characters listed here are definitely fictitious, and any resemblance to actual individuals is not intended. In fact, I would expect that if an elected officeholder would see himself or herself in this chapter, she or he would not want to admit it! So here are some characters for my sitcom. The meanings of their names are listed in parenthesis.*

---

*Authors Note: None of the names have been taken from real life or lives of anyone I know is real. They have been taken from *The Writer's Digest Character Naming Source Book* by Sherilyn Kenyon with Hal Blythe and Charlie Sweet. There are more male than female names because the balance of female to male on councils is still short of females.

THE SITCOM

• **Gerhard Gerlach** (Hard Spear, Spear Thrower) — Uses words as weapons; has no qualms about verbally cutting down staff or colleagues publicly with criticism. He takes pleasure in asking questions that will surely embarrass the target person because the unfortunate target-du-jour can't possibly have ready answers and could not have done the needed research to produce a proper response.

• **Rasmus Shipton** (Amiable, From the Sheep Farm) — Wants to be everyone's friend; wants to be reelected; wants never to make a decision that will upset anyone; abstains instead from voting when issues are very controversial and ends up pleasing nobody and gains a reputation for being indecisive.

• **Haduwig Twein** (Strife, Cut in Two) — As indecisive as Rasmus Shipton, Haduwig is conflicted about voting any issue because of promises made during the campaign. When the welfare of the whole city is in conflict with what a roomful of angry citizens is demanding, Haduwig abstains from voting due to conflict of interest, which is the truth because Haduwig's conflict is the inability to make a decision under duress, and her interest, like Rasmus Shipton's main interest, is in wanting to be reelected. But Haduwig is female and so people say, "Isn't that just like a woman? She can't make up her mind." And women who have worked most of their lives to attain equality with men wish that instead of running for political office, Haduwig had taken up a hobby like painting by numbers, which does not involve making decisions!

• **Rickman Sterne** (Powerful, Austere) — No matter how much anything costs, Sterne says it's too much and launches into a diatribe about reckless spending; how things were cheaper 25 years ago; how government spending is out of hand; how we must all tighten our belts; how we should do more with less; and cliché after cliché about too much and too costly. A disruption to any budget-planning meeting, Sterne wants more services from less money and has no suggestions about how to accomplish the impossible. Sterne is especially concerned about raises for city staff who, in his opinion, spend too much time chatting and taking breaks. As luck would have it, it is always someone like Sterne who drives past public works road workers while they are taking a lunch break on the job or waiting for a cement truck. He sees them not working and complains that all street projects are behind schedule because those public works guys just sit around instead of doing their jobs.

• **Nyle Stillmann** (Island, Quiet) — A quiet loner, Stillmann says little, therefore neither annoys nor encourages anybody; always avoids controversy; usually seconds motions but rarely makes them; and gets reelected, usually because Stillmann can be relied upon to always show up and not aggravate anyone. Stillmann hates a roll call vote because, if the truth be known, he really just moves his lips when council votes verbally. People like him because he is not a threat and because he and his vote are predictable; that is to say innocuous!

• **Osric Strang** (Divine Ruler, Powerful) — Strang is always in charge of everything. Everything must be done the Strang way or no way. Strang is the powerful, possibly divine, ruler who knows all, sees all, and demands all. You know when Strang is at city hall because all the staff doors are closed or staff has mysteriously disappeared. At social functions and public events, colleagues wait for Strang to be seated so that they can sit somewhere else. People who understand how to deal with a bully deal with Strang by manipulation. If Strang has been manipulated into thinking an idea is a Strang Plan, it's a good thing and Strang will make it happen — his way, of course! Strang struts into meetings as if he owns the place; glad hands everyone as if he is knighting them;

brings his supporters to council meetings to cheer for his arguments and support his pronouncements or at least nod their heads when Strang voices an opinion. Strang is a power junkie and sincerely believes that the city will go to hell in a handbasket if he ever stays away from holding office for too long. Since he exudes self-confidence and strong leadership, people reelect Strang, much to the dismay of those who would like to have peaceful cooperation among staff and council. He is also disliked by those who want to be like Strang but are not Strang-like enough to usurp his power until he decides to give it up. And Strang will give up power when donkeys fly and hell freezes over. The interesting thing is that because of his experience, he is competent and would be a greater source for good if he were not so intent upon being the boss of the GOBS.

• **Aloisia Ulrike** (Famous Fighting Woman, Mistress of All) — The original Queen Bee, she has been president of every women's organization in town and is accustomed to having things go her way or no way. If Aloisia Ulrike and Osrick Strang end up on the same board, council, or committee, fireworks start and never stop. Everything that Strang is, Ulrike is too. The difference is that the people who say that Strang is a decisive and dynamic leader will say that Ulrike's leadership qualifies her to get a title that begins with a letter close to the beginning of the alphabet, before the "d" in decisive and dynamic . . . as in "b."

• **Wyndham Valiant** (From the Windy Village, Brave) — Never the brightest bulb in the chandelier, Valiant runs for election for reasons known only in the deepest recesses of the Valiant brain. Valiant gets "pity votes" from sympathetic friends who think such a person will never be elected anyway; they are always stunned and surprised when pity votes tally up to a win. Valiant tries to learn but is really just not up to the job. People shake their heads and mutter the word "What?" a lot when he votes, which is sometimes against things he has spoken for and for things he has spoken against. Valiant is nice fellow but even nice guys can end up in the wrong place at the wrong time.

• **Wenda Maida** (Comely, Maiden) — Former beauty queen, she really runs for office so that she can sit on a dais and wear nice clothes. She often dresses in what has to be called a "costume" because she believes that she should present herself as a "colorful character." She is usually harmless and is likely to serve just one term, because after she's worn all her costumes she gets bored with the whole concept of government — especially those occasions when you have to wear a business suit.

• **Ubel Webbestre** (Evil, Weaver) — Webbestre weaves tangled webs of rumors that hurt good people, especially those who may have wronged Webbestre or a Webbestre supporter/friend/relative. Webbestre never forgets and never passes up an opportunity to avenge real or perceived evil with the Webbestre truth-bending tales of woe. Anyone who opposes Webbestre in an election will have an opponent forever — at council meetings, at social events, in fact at any gathering, Webbestre will find some way to compete and vanquish former opponents even if it's as silly as buying the last hot dog on the grill at a city picnic. His glee is so amusing that former opponents let him win just to see him react.

• **Collis Bardick** (Son of the Dark Man, Ax Ruler) — Comes from a small town "ruling family" and believes it is his birthright to get elected. His theme is: "If my daddy did it I can too, and the way my daddy did it is the way it should always be and so let's not change anything." People may snicker behind Bardick's back saying, "His daddy kept all the brains in that family and didn't pass 'em down." Bardick brings his children to meetings to groom them for continuance of the Bardick dynasty. And, most of the time, a Bardick is harmless unless a Bardick marries a Strang or an Ulrike and produces a bully who is totally stuck in the past!

• **Elethia Helma** (Healer, Protective) — Fancies herself to be the peacemaker and operates with passive aggression. Her game is to get agreement to all of her issues and she often gets support because nobody wants to appear mean to such a sweet lady. The Open Meetings Act is something she just can't consider. She's always on the phone calling people to get their support for her projects and issues. She gets other people to make motions and second them so that she never appears assertive. If she gets backed into a corner from which escape can only be made with a decisive motion, she moves to table the issue or idea for further study, thus avoiding any possible conflict. The next day she is back on the phone getting her forces to set up the action for her. She can cause dissention among councilmembers who may not know that they are being manipulated.

• **Willa Tugenda** (Resolute, Virtue) — Long a community activist, Willa has many causes and uses the city to promote them, whether or not the whole city benefits and whether or not the majority of citizens agree with her causes. Her male counterpart is Derwin Tedmund. Peculiar things happen when Tugenda and Tedmund work together and sometimes good happens and other times the not-all-good happens.

• **Derwin Tedmund** (Friend of the Deer, National Protector) — Has good ideas but implements them in ways that aggravate others. Derwin plunges ahead before he gathers the means and modes of accomplishing a project or promoting a cause and never lets facts get in the way of his steamroller techniques. He is always baffled when people don't agree with his ideas because he believes that if it's his idea, and he means well, it has to be a good thing. Tugenda and Tedmund tend to polarize groups and cause divisiveness because people either totally support them or vehemently oppose them on principle.

• **Sunny Madre** (Cheerful, Mother) — Brings everyone home-baked cookies and cakes, always remembers everyone's birthday, straightens men's ties and women's collars before a meeting, and generally mothers everyone. For these sacrifices, she expects that people will agree with everything she says because not to would be like disrespecting one's own mom. She is a positive-thinking buffer between all of the others and can be counted on to defuse explosions before they happen — a one-woman bomb squad. Her kindness, when it's genuine and not manipulative like Helma's mode, can be a great benefit to a difficult council. She gets reelected because people like nice; it's a relief from the un-nice!

The Meeting from Government Hell

Imagine a city council budget workshop at which the council is deciding its priorities for the coming fiscal year. Mayor Collis Bardick is presiding. There is an unusually large crowd to observe the workshop because Ubel Webbestre has told his neighbors that the council will raise their property taxes in the coming year due to the inclusion of too many frills in the budget.

One of those frills is a proposal from Wenda Maida, who wants to buy matching shirts for the council to wear to the next TML conference, just like several other cities' councilmembers wore at the last TML. They could also wear the shirts to city events so that everyone could recognize the councilmembers.

Another frill has been proposed by Sunny Madre; she wants to give all city employees a five percent across-the-board raise in salary in addition to the usual cost-of-living increae. Yet another frill, according to Webbestre, is a project proposed by Willa Tugenda and Derwin Tedmund. They want to build a skateboard park because other cities have them and each of them has a son who skateboards.

As soon as the meeting begins, Rickman Sterne objects to having the city purchase shirts for councilmembers. He says that they are too expensive and councilmembers who want shirts should buy their own. He also objects to the city employees' raise. They had a raise three years ago; he hasn't had a raise on his job so why should they get more money? He says that the skateboard park project doesn't deserve comment; it is just too expensive to build and insure, and who wants all those kids from other cities coming to use our city's facilities? It's bad enough that the park is full of people from outside of the city who are picnicking every Sunday, barbecuing and hogging the picnic tables, not to mention monopolizing the children's play area and using the restrooms.

Osric Strang tells Mayor Bardick to declare all of the speakers out of order since the city manager has not yet presented the projected income and general expenses for the coming year. He doesn't want to talk about shirts, employee benefits, or skateboarding at this time. Aloisia Ulrike agrees and adds that nobody has asked for her opinion about the color of the shirts and blue is her favorite color. Strang says the color doesn't matter; the topic is out of order. Wyndam Valiant says he wouldn't mind talking about the shirts but he is concerned about the skateboard park's location, and by the way he would wear an X-Large shirt if they are knit. Gerhard Gerlach comments that Valiant probably needs an XX-Large. Elethia Helma says she's certain an X-Large will do for Valiant since the shirts are quality knit and won't shrink.

Mayor Bardick asks the city manager to begin the budget presentation. The city manager is interrupted by Gerlach who wants to know if staff has information about employee raises in all other cities of the area. Staff members say they can provide the information but it will take some time to get it. Also, there is a problem because each of the cities has its own titles for the different job categories which makes comparing the salaries for specific jobs difficult.

Sterne says he is sure that several, actually most, of the city employees are overpaid and the whole pay structure should be over-hauled to bring city salaries in line; he doesn't say in line with what, just "in line."

Strang says that the time to discuss salary increases is after the department heads give their presentations. He says that everyone is out of order again. He tells Bardick to use his gavel so they can proceed in an orderly manner.

Mayor Bardick is beginning to wish that he were somewhere else.

The budget presentation goes on. An estimated $6.8 million is to be considered. Each department head presents its plans for the year and each is interrupted by Gerlach asking for statistics that are not readily available without research. How many miles of streets do other cities renovate each year? What is the average number of police officers and firefighters employed by other cities of comparable size? The statistics about cost-of-living salary increases are available but Gerlach doesn't believe them. Sterne holds fast to his belief that since he has not received a substantial raise in his paying job, city employees do not need a 5 percent raise. A compromise is finally reached so that city employees will get a cost-of-living increase which will be about 2.5 percent but no other salary increases. Unfortunately, the city employees' share of the group health insurance plan has increased by 2.5 percent and so the city employees will be getting no real raise at all. Only Sunny Madre sees this as an injustice. She resolves to bake more cookies for the employees' break room as compensation.

Since money was saved on the city employee raise, Tugenda and Tedmund bring up the construction of a skateboard park as feasible. Staff, aware that the skateboard park issue would come up, has done some research and advises council that liability insurance will cost about $10,000 a year, if an insurer can be found; costs for the skateboard ramps and for fences around the ramps to keep out small children can be upwards of $50,000, with the final cost to be determined by the design. It is noted that hiring at least one staff person to monitor the skateboarders' activities will add to the annual budget for employee salaries and benefits since constant supervision of the skateboarders is required by insurance companies.

Sterne is outraged! He is opposed to the project. Gerlach agrees. He says it's a half-baked idea cooked up by a couple of kooks.

Mayor Bardick seriously wishes he were somewhere else — anywhere else.

Tugenda and Tedmund believe that parents would supervise the skateboarders as volunteers. Neither staff nor other councilmembers believe that volunteers can be relied upon to supervise every hour that the park is open. Tugenda and Tedmund don't believe that there would be a lot of insurance claims for injuries because the kids would be careful, and that a skateboard park could be built economically if volunteers would do some of the work. Tugenda knows a neighbor who has done cement walkways in his garden and thinks he would help with constructing the ramps and maintaining them.

Helma wants to table the issue until more research can be done but Strang and Ulrike, who had not been consulted about the park by Tugenda and Tedmund before the budget meeting, want the project to be abandoned. Ulrike says she has seen Tugenda's neighbor's garden sidewalk and it has a crack. Besides, a sidewalk is nothing like a skateboarding ramp. The others agree. The issue is tabled indefinitely.

Shipton, Twein, and Stillman are relieved that they didn't have to vote on the issue. Stillman is especially relieved because he knows that if he voted for the skateboard park a lot of citizens will be angry, and if he voted against the park, his two children, who also skateboard, would make his home life as miserable as his public life. He is thinking that he won't run for reelection to any office ever again.

Undaunted by council objections, Tugenda and Tedmund hope to bring it up another year, perhaps when Strang and Ulrike are not on council. And they decide that the next time they want to bring up the skateboard park at council, they will get together at the Dairy Queen with whoever replaces Strang and Ulrike to get their support before the meeting. They conclude that the Open Meetings Act is for other cities, not theirs.

Maida still wants the city to buy the councilmembers' shirts and says if they don't like knit golf shirts, denim would be as attractive. Discussion bogs down in the selection of the color for knit shirts and whether or not denim would be as attractive. Valiant says he's sure an X-Large will fit him and agrees that Helma is right when she says that the shirts won't shrink if they get quality knits. He thinks that he needs a Large in denim. Helma suggests they table the issue until more information can be found about knit versus denim. Everyone but Maida agrees; it is getting late and the ballgame is on TV at 8:30 p.m.

Mayor Bardick takes a deep breath in relief that the session is over. He sets the date for another budget workshop and the session ends. He notes that in his father's day skateboards were not an issue, and he would probably wear a Medium if the shirts are quality knits; he's not sure what size in denim. He likes blue.

The mayor's son, Junior Bardick, and daughter, Bubbette Bardick, are in the audience observing democracy at work, as they do at all council meetings. Their dad wants them to prepare themselves for their roles in the Bardick dynasty.

Junior whispers to Bubbette, "When I am mayor, I will get a bigger gavel."

Bubbette rolls her eyes and replies, "With guys it's always size."

The newspaper reports on the budget workshop.

Outraged citizens write letters to the editor saying that councilmembers' shirts and skateboarding should not have priority over street and sidewalk repair, or police and fire protection.

Some letters to the editor say that employee raises should be "kept in line" (again, no determination of what line) and others say employees deserve raises so that good employees can be retained and not hired away by cities that pay more.

Other letter-writers say the city should buy shirts for employees so that they have a uniform appearance, but councilmembers should pay for their own shirts.

Skateboarders write in to say they have no place to skate except in places that are too dangerous or where the cops shag them away. No parents volunteer to supervise a skateboard park. Several people write letters to the editor and call city hall with complaints about rude and noisy behavior of skateboarders on city streets and sidewalks.

One person writes a letter to the editor expressing disgust over the focus of the budget discussion, saying there are more important issues than shirts and skateboarding. He calls for more people to run for council who have a better grasp of what is, or what should be, priorities for the city. The letter-writer says that it's people like the ones on the current council that keep him from voting. He declares that everyone in politics is totally nuts! He says that the city is going to hell in a handbasket and it's all the council's fault!

Despite the citizen's predictions of doom and the council's disagreements, the budget gets adopted at the appropriate time with each department's allocation in the budget remaining the same as the previous year. The budget includes only the meaningless cost-of-living raise for employees (due to the increase health insurance payments) and no across-the-board salary boost. Also, the budget does not include a skateboard park, and, to Maida's dismay, it does not include any shirts — quality knit or otherwise — for anybody.

Mayor Bardick believes his daddy would be pleased since nothing really has changed since his daddy's administration, except for more money in the budget. He is a bit disappointed that he didn't get a shirt with "Mayor" embroidered on it but there is always another year, another budget, and another workshop, perhaps with different people on council.

Ever optimistic, Bardick hopes that councils will be more agreeable when his son, Junior, is mayor and his daughter, Bubbette, is a councilmember.

However, considering the past, and with concern for the future of his family's city, he makes a mental note to have staff buy a bigger mayor's gavel. Junior will need all the help he can get!

Chapter 10:

How Not to Be a Sitcom

Numerous publications (e.g., "Guide for City Councilmembers" published by The Texas Department of Housing and Community Affairs Local Government Services) are offered by various organizations, such as Councils of Governments and Municipal Leagues, which explain the laws governing political campaigns, officeholding, and the other legal aspects of politics. Laws change frequently so publications can go out-of-date between elections; make sure to get a recent copy. However, although legalities change, certain basic rules do not change. and those who don't bother to learn the basics or who choose to ignore them either get into trouble or cause it for others. If enough basic rule-breakers sit on the same dais, the result is the kind of chaos that inspires TV sitcoms, drives the paid staff balmy, and draws the ire of voters.

Dealing with a City Manager and Staff

Most Texas cities have the city manager form of government in which the function of the mayor and the councilmembers is to set policy and the city manager's job is to carry out those policies. To compare the system with business, it's as if the council is the board of trustees, the mayor is the chairman of the board, and the city manager is the chief executive officer of the corporation. The council and mayor hire the city manager and in some cases also approve the chief of police selected by the city manager. The city manager is responsible for hiring and firing all employees, for producing a budget that accommodates the goals set by the council, and for carrying out any other policies and tasks as directed by the mayor and council. Since the city manager serves at the pleasure of the council, the council's power over the city manager is that it can fire one who does not please them. Contracts with city managers differ but most have a clause in which the city manager gets six months or one year's salary if terminated due to council's displeasure.

Just about every Texas Municipal League conference I ever attended had at least one course on dealing with the city manager and city staff, which should be an indication that people need help in this phase of city government. One of the first causes of problems with a city manager, according to several speakers, is that in city manager form of government you have people with less expertise in government (especially the newly elected officials) supervising a person who has greater expertise than they have, and to complicate matters, also probably makes more money in the job than the councilmembers make in their paid jobs. (Note: While some Texas cities and cities in other states pay salaries and benefits to elected officials, most pay no salary; some pay a small stipend per meeting. It amazes people from outside of Texas that anyone would work a 20- to 30-hour week, as many smalltown mayors do, for no salary at all!)

To make the situation even more complicated, many councilmembers come on board with an adversarial attitude toward city staff in general and the city manager in particular. Instead of recognizing the city manager's and other staffers' expertise, some councilmembers seem to resent it and make life miserable with constant criticism of staff under the guise of reform, whether or not reform is really needed. In my opinion, most (but one supposes not all) wouldn't behave as adversaries in their paid jobs and would try to work with people respectfully to maintain harmony and progress without pain.

Sometimes it's not an adversarial attitude but a lack of consideration that causes councilmembers to act inappropriately toward city managers and staff. For example, when a councilmember has a question about some item on the meeting's agenda, it's best to ask the city manager *before* the meeting so that the manager and/or staff can get the answers prepared. Blindsiding the city manager or staff publicly is awkward for everyone. Questions can come up during discussion that one didn't anticipate while reading the packet prior to the meeting, but whenever possible it's only fair to give staff time to research and come up with the right information. If a councilmember or mayor thinks that others on the council should have that same information, the question can be asked again in session and then the city manager or staff person can answer it again so that all have the same information.

Often, mayors and councilmembers step out of the policy-making role and bypass the city manager by directly micro-managing the city departments instead of following a chain of command in which they deal with the city manager and the city manager deals with the different departments' directors and staff. If there is a problem in any of the departments, the city manager, who hires and fires people in the departments, needs to know about it anyway; so the proper procedure is to go to the city manager's office first. Of course the city manager must respond to the councilmember and act appropriately to fix the problem.

The May 2004 issue of "Public Management" offers "Six Reasons Why It's Best To Work Through The Manager" from the city manager point of view:*

• 1. Councilmembers should work through the city manager because city managers cannot be on top of things if they don't know what the things are. While staff members can relay to the manager information given them by councilmembers, such secondhand information certainly raises the chance of miscommunication.

• 2. Council should work through the manager because bypassing the manager may give the impression that there is a problem in the council-manager relationship and this impression reflects badly on both the manager and the council. This perception can undermine the manager's credibility within the organization and the respect that staff feels for the councilmember. Staff may think council doesn't want to work with or doesn't trust the manager. Staff also may think that the councilmember doesn't play by the rules and is seeking special treatment. Bypassing the manager also gives the impression that it's okay for staff to go around the manager because council does it.

• 3. It's not possible for managers to treat all councilmembers equally if the manager is unaware of the treatment that one councilmember is getting from staff. Managers must seek to give all councilmembers equal treatment that includes giving them the same information, same levels of support, and same accessibility to staff in general. When it's a request for staff work, the manager needs to judge if the request is consistent with council policy and/or if full council should direct such work. When requests are not always made through the manager, inequities may come up over time.

*Article by Ken Hampian, City Manager of San Luis Obispo, CA

• 4. Councilmembers are often perceived as having "awesome power," and so direct requests to staff can lead to surprising and negative unintended consequences. For example, a councilmember's simple request for information can be interpreted by staff as a direct order to do something that was never intended by other councilmembers. This happens especially when direct contacts are made with staff below the department head level. Councilmembers may not know they have that much power but to lower level staff, who seldom have contact with the mayor or councilmembers, councilmembers are "higher-ups" to whom staff must respond.

• 5. Direct councilmember contact with staff members below the department head level boosts the likelihood of getting erroneous or incomplete information. The farther down the ladder the councilmember goes to get information, the more likely it will come from someone who is less familiar with the situation's or issue's "big picture." The manager is the person with one-stop service who can produce more complete information.

• 6. Direct councilmember contact also can inadvertently cause awkward, embarrassing situations for the staff member involved. For example, if a councilmember gets incomplete or erroneous information from a lower level staff person, the staffer is embarrassed and may be perceived as undermining the department head or manager's position.

Dealing with Colleagues

Respecting one's colleagues when you don't necessarily agree with them or don't even like them is a challenge. But the main rule is that you can and should disagree without becoming disagreeable. Once elected, you owe the citizens a certain degree of proper decorum during public meetings and events, even if citizens may be temporarily entertained by a lack of decorum on the part of their elected officials. Eventually, the entertainment value of poorly behaved councilmembers degenerates into disgust and distrust, and unacceptable behaviors reflect badly even on those who maintain their dignity on the dais.

Robert's Rules of Order are valuable but my observation is that sometimes people get so hung up on the rules that they forget common sense. For example, every now and then the rules make things more complicated than anything ought to be. At a meeting I attended, a motion was made and seconded; discussion resulted in an amendment and a second to the amendment, which resulted in yet another amendment to the previous amendment and second to that amendment, which resulted in a most confusing discussion of *Robert's Rules of Order* and even more confusing display of voting on amendments, seconds, and withdrawing amendments and seconds. By the time the mayor called for a vote on the original motion, it appeared that several bewildered councilmembers were not sure what they were voting for or against. Worse yet, the business person requesting the zoning decision didn't understand if his request was approved or not and so a staff person had to take him out of chambers to explain. Citizens in the audience were guffawing loudly at the whole procedure and some walked out shaking their heads; it definitely looked like a TV sitcom. It would have been simpler if everyone were asked to withdraw their motions and seconds and start all over again. The rule of common sense has to prevail when people get all tangled up in the other rules.

In my opinion, there isn't much you can do with someone who has decided to be difficult. When you have to deal with cantankerous councilmembers, the concept of "you can't change people but you can change how you react to them" is useful. The easiest thing to do is to agree that whatever Councilmember Cantankerous says needs to be said. Note that I didn't say agree with *what* Cantankerous said, only that it *can* be said. Getting angry solves nothing and only contributes to an already hostile situation. It helps if you don't have the kind of ego that needs to be right all of the time. Most of us have had a boss at one time or other who was wrong only once — the time that he thought he was wrong. Most nasty people eventually shoot themselves in the foot, and then if they have been way too nasty, somebody, some-time, and somewhere, will kick their crutches away so as to totally neutralize them.

Lyle Sumek is one of my favorite speakers at TML meetings. At one of his sessions he referred to a category of elected official he calls a "mom" who, like a real mom, never forgets anything. He noted that this type of "mom" can be male or female. Anyone who has run for public office knows the type of "mom" who loses an election and then adopts a personal vendetta against the person who won. And, of course, there are the folks who have real or imagined reasons to have vendettas against people they believe have insulted them.

I recall a council meeting while I was mayor in which a mom-type person wanted to speak during the last Citizens to be Heard section of the agenda. As the person was speaking, I was handed a note from the police dispatcher that said I should stop the meeting immediately and clear the building because the weather service said a severe hailstorm was headed directly toward the city and that it possibly included tornadoes. I said, "Excuse me," to the speaker, read the note aloud, and asked for a motion to adjourn.

"But I want to talk," the person demanded. This same person had demanded to speak out of order at a previous meeting and so was irked at having to stop speaking yet again.

"But I have to get everyone out of here and home before the storm hits," I said, pointing out that it was a matter of public safety.

The person continued to demand to speak, saying, "I don't know what that note says but I want to talk."

So I used the gavel and adjourned the meeting. I arrived at my house and had just pulled into my garage when the storm hit the city; it was a huge storm with strong winds and large hail. I hoped that others arrived home on time and that the verbose speaker would understand. Not so — I made an enemy who later ran for council because of the perceived "insult" of being silenced and never failed to announce at every opportunity that the mayor didn't let people speak at meetings.

Dealing with Citizens at Meetings

Most recently, government educational conference speakers have been referring to "servant leadership." My definition of "servant leadership" is leadership/officeholding in which those who are elected focus on serving the people, not themselves or their own special interests. Mayors and councilmembers must always consider what is best for the city as a whole, not just the thirty-five or so people who are taking turns at the podium demanding that one cause or another be given priority and that council should vote as they say, even if one neighborhood would benefit at the expense of other areas of the city.

In one of his how-to-govern sessions, Sumek warned councilmembers that you will always have to deal with that ever-present group of negative thinkers — about 20% of the population — who are generally the most vocal. They operate under the "squeaky wheel gets the grease" principle but they shout instead of squeak. They resist change and see it as painful, disruptive, and destructive and they need to be convinced that change isn't bad. To effect change you need to show the negative thinkers that the changes being proposed will mean new benefits. You will need the help of those in the population who are truly positive thinkers — another 20% — and you will need to reach the 40% or so of people in the population who don't really care. Sometimes, as I've noted in Chapter 5, no matter how hard you try to communicate, you can't get support.

Considered by many people to be the dean of city attorneys in Texas, Harvey L. Hardy has written a memoir entitled *a Lifetime at the Bar, a Lawyer's Memoir.**

In his entertaining book, he writes about an "unbelievable" budget controversy over the salary of a San Antonio city manager that led to huge repercussions in other city situations and eventually to the council being put out of office at the next election. Appraising the result of the controversy and the reactions of the public to it, Hardy said in his book,

> The biggest drawback to democracy is the intermittent phenomena of half-baked mass hysteria over issues of little or no importance in a well-balanced scheme of things.

I don't think anyone could say it better than Hardy has. It certainly is something to think about when you are sitting on the dais and trying to make a decision after fifty-seven of your fellow citizens have berated you and your colleagues on the council for your past, present, and future actions on behalf of the city.

Whether it's in a public hearing or during the Citizens to be Heard section of the meeting, the mayor has to continue to control the meeting fairly so that everyone gets a chance to speak, with no

---

* Vantage Press, Inc., N.Y., 1999.

one person dominating. Some cities (school boards, county courts) have time limits such as three or five minutes for speakers who must sign up to speak. When a very large number of people want to speak on a controversial issue, the mayor can allow some people to relinquish their times to be used by the spokesperson of their group if there is such a person.

One way to save time when you are in charge of a meeting is to tell the people who wish to speak that you will read two names, the name of the speaker who will go to the podium first and the name of the next speaker, who is asked to cue up behind the one at the podium, ready to speak when the first speaker is finished. This saves the time wasted while people walk from their chairs to the podium. It also keeps people in the audience from muttering to each other during the lull and order is better maintained.

Someone once told me that the main accomplishment of almost all organized protests is to annoy the people who are not participating in them. When I was mayor, I tended to discourage audience applause and other reactions aimed at speakers for or against issues — I'd ask for order, respect, and courtesy, and use the gavel to get it. When a large crowd was anticipated for a controversial agenda item, we'd ask the police chief and/or extra officers to be present.

It seemed to me that most of the controversies occur when property owners are requesting permits and zoning changes. At such times, it seems that people forget or don't want to acknowledge that all property owners have some rights. A person who has invested thousands, and in some cases millions of dollars, in a piece of real estate should be able to realize some benefit from the investment just as a homeowner has a right to certain quality of life amenities. Most often, compromises are possible although we all recognize that in compromise everyone loses something and everyone wins something and most of the time not everyone thinks the deal is fair.

Sometimes things seem fair during negotiations and discussions but in practice they are not. For example, I have regrets about only one vote in my ten years on council and it was during one of my first meetings. It was a case in which an auto dealer needed to expand car storage area into land that the dealer already owned. This piece of land backed up against a single dwelling neighborhood and the homeowners protested about lights on the car lot and noise and just having the business on the other side of a fence. The property was properly zoned and the compromise was that a fence would be built and landscaping trees, etc., would be planted as a buffer between the business and the homeowner's property. It was one of my first meetings and it seemed fair to me. When I checked on the property a couple of years later, when the landscaping should have had time to grow, I learned that the fence was chain link and the homeowner's view from the backyard was a bunch of cars — not very scenic. We had not specified privacy or barrier fencing nor had we required more concealing landscaping.

A couple of years later, a situation arose when a national gas station chain with mini-grocery wanted to build a new facility on the corner of a street that was one of the main entries into a subdivision and which backed up to the subdivision. Council chambers overflowed with citizens protesting the project because they feared it would increase traffic in their subdivision, would have lighting that was offensive to homeowners nearby, and would generally be a nuisance to the neighborhood. Council got the gas station project manager to hold meetings with the neighbors and several compromises were reached. The gas station would put up a privacy fence a foot higher than the usual height city ordinance required and plant shrubbery on the neighborhood side of the fence to disguise it; it would install downward-focused lighting. After it was built, the station did not increase traffic in the subdivision, the residents liked the convenience of the mini-grocery, and during a gas price war it had the cheapest gas in the county. I had many positive comments from the same people who had protested. The lesson here was that compromise can work.

Dealing with Citizens' Complaints

It is the job of the mayor, I think, to return all phone calls, unless there is some legal situation going on and then I think it is best to have the city manager or city attorney respond. Giving a wrong answer is always possible when passing on complicated information. Always remember the childhood game of "secret" in which each person whispers into another's ear to relay a story told by a first person. By the time the story gets to the last person, it is almost always unrecognizable!

Whenever a citizen complains about any situation or city employee, it's always best to get more information about the situation and to get the other side of the issue if it's an employee complaint before making any judgments. As noted elsewhere in this book, city employees may become targets when people are really angry about city policies and/or ordinances because they are the messengers. This is especially true in matters regarding permits, zoning, and traffic offenses.

For example, a business owner called to complain about the city inspector causing all sorts of inconveniences and extra expenses. It seems that the business owner had a concrete slab poured over various utilities and plumbing installations before getting a permit and/or proper inspection. The city inspector, following the state law, said that he couldn't inspect things that were under cement, and so an engineer's certificate ensuring that all state codes were observed was required before the project could pass inspection. The business owner shouted so loudly I had to hold the phone away from my ear, but shouting louder was not the solution — state law had to be observed.

In another chapter, I have written about the young teen who was ticketed for speeding and complained about the police officer treating him rudely. The cop sternly lectured him in addition to the ticket because the boy was speeding/tailgating behind an ambulance which was transporting a patient to the hospital. The boy was endangering the patient as well as speeding and the officer let him know it. Also, the boy had received many tickets and the mother had told our cops that she would take away his car keys if he had another, which accounts for the boy trying to get out of being charged.

Often the person making the complaint doesn't really have all the facts and sometimes the complaint is in no way valid. For example, about two-thirds of the City of Leon Valley is serviced by the Leon Valley Water System and about one third (generally the older neighborhoods) by the San Antonio Water System. A couple of weeks after San Antonio citizens approved the addition of fluoride to their drinking water, a Leon Valley citizen called me to complain, "Our water just doesn't taste good anymore since those people in San

Antonio voted to put fluoride in it." When I politely told the citizen, "Sir, although the vote was this year, the fluoride won't be added until next year," there was dead silence on the line.

Sometimes a complaint is very difficult to understand. Throughout our city we have drainage ditches that run under sidewalks. Where this situation occurs, the part of the sidewalk over the ditch is elevated to form a small bridge so that people can stay dry or relatively dry in a gullywasher. One citizen complained that one of these little bridges enabled passersby to stand higher and thereby see into that citizen's backyard and that the bridge should be flattened. The cost to the city would be about one to two thousand dollars and then water would wash over the sidewalk when the ditch was full. I knew this because I made several trips to see how the water flowed when it rained. I also tried to see into the person's yard while standing on the little bridge and watched to see if anyone else ever stood on the bridge to peep into the person's yard. Actually, after many trips I never saw anyone walking on that sidewalk. I was really baffled as to why the city should spend $1000-plus to tear down something functional because somebody felt "watched", when there were so many other uses for that money. After repeated complaints, we put the project on the public works list but couldn't in good conscience give it as high a priority as other public works projects.

Dealing with Different Age Groups

As previously noted, Lyle Sumek is a frequent speaker at TML meetings. One of his seminars deals with the ways different age groups tend to think and to interact with each other. He says that different age groups bring different experiences to the council table and so their actions and reactions will reflect their experiences.

• The first group, whom he calls the OFs for Old Fogies, are people who were born before 1935. Shaped by the Great Depression and World War II, they respect authority, have a work ethic, are frugal stewards of public dollars, and their favorite question is "How much does that cost?" They very often base their decisions on cost and are not always easy to convince when a project is presented.

• The next group, whom he calls the Rejectionists, were born between 1947 and 1954. They grew up with TV, Viet Nam, and tend to be cynical. They may have no respect for authority and their favorite question is "Why are we doing it this way?" They ask a lot of questions and annoy the OFs. They want people to be involved and participate; will spend money for quality; want balance of work and family in their lifestyle and will put this value before attending meetings, which also annoys the OFs.

• The third group, called Tweeners by Sumek, are confusing to both the OFs and the Rejectionists. Brought up in the forties and fifties, which were times of change and opportunity, they love a challenge and will plunge in to do a job. They grew up practicing how to avoid nuclear annihilation. They are goal-directed and believe in "we" power. Teamwork comes from this group especially, and they share their enthusiasm for the team concept with the OFs and Rejectionists.

• The fourth group, called the Hedonistic-Traditionalists by Sumek, were born between 1954 and 1967. They tend to dress casually for council meetings (even in shorts and T-shirts) which annoys the OFs. They grew up in constant crisis, with Kennedy's and King's assassinations, Viet Nam, inflation. They hate long meetings and want to get on with it. They will work hard but party hard afterwards. Unlike the other groups, they prefer to socialize with friends and not their fellow councilmembers, which also annoys the OFs.

• The fifth group, which Sumek calls the Boomerangers, were born after 1967. They have goals, but grew up in quiet times when

life was easier. They are not in a hurry and their favorite question
is "What's the big deal?" Their lax time frame annoys other age
groups which are more goal-oriented.

After attending several sessions with Sumek, I began to recognize
the different age groups and their behaviors as shown by both councilmembers and citizens, but it seemed to me that the age for the
groups was often an attitude more than it was a chronological age and
that some people are OFs at any age, which almost guarantees them a
lifetime of being annoyed with every other group. We do have to
respect the different groups and cultures which we are elected to
represent, and understanding them surely helps us to deal with them.

Dealing with the Media

I had been a reporter covering the same city council on which I
served as councilmember and later as mayor. One thing I learned
early on and which I told all of my fellow media friends is this: It is
much easier to write an editorial about what government needs to do
or needs not to do than it is to actually cause good things to happen.
But every now and then you will get a good idea, and with the help of
all sorts of other people, it will benefit the public in a significant way,
especially if you are able to get the wheels of government to turn
more quickly than normal.

However, when dealing with the media as a public official, you
become very cautious when talking about ideas. If you think aloud, as
in "I think that we really need to build a new fire station," the story
may come out that your city is building a new fire station, the impli-
cation being that it will happen tomorrow or next week.

When I was a reporter in the good old days, I always believed that
when someone said something was off the record that it was not to be

in the story. I really don't think that rule applies anymore. Just about everything you say will be "on the record" in some way or other and you just pray that the record is accurate. I came to believe that to be interviewed is to be misquoted. When I was a reporter, I found that a lot of people did not remember what they had said. I would have information in my notes and the speaker would recall nothing about it. However, sometimes reporters don't read their notes accurately. I have been quoted in quotation marks — not just paraphrased — with words that are not even in my vocabulary. I have been misquoted even when the reporter took so-called quotes from printed copy that I provided. A good example was the speech I made when announcing that I would not seek a fourth term as mayor. I carefully crafted the speech so that my reasons for not running would be understood and passed out copies to the reporters. One paper "quoted" me and in doing so, distorted the meaning of several statements.

One of my favorite misquotes was an interview I did with a reporter who was writing a feature story about a former mayor, my mentor, Mayor Ken Alley, who had been named our city's Paragon Home Town Hero. The gentleman was in his late eighties at the time and I said that he was "very spry" and worked out at our local gym. The story said that he was "very strong" (which is not the same as spry) and that he "worked out at the gym three times a week." I had no idea how many times a week he went to the gym and so I could not have said that. Of course a feature like this has no repercussions but being misquoted about city business can cause a lot of trouble.

I did misquote someone while I was a reporter but the misquote was a result of my not being a native Texan. The story was about sewer lines going into a subdivision, and at that time each councilmember had a city department as responsibility. At the meeting I covered, the cost to homeowners of connecting to the new sewer line was given and I called the councilmember responsible for public works for verification. In his Texas accent, he said it would cost "fortasix" dollars a foot to connect, which on the phone sounded to me, a transplanted Texan, as "forty-six dollars" but which was really "four to six dollars" a foot. City Hall and the poor councilmember were deluged with complaint calls from citizens outraged at the cost of connection to sewer lines. We printed a retraction and I apologized but complaints continued for a long time.

Dealing with Government Business

Often people run for office saying that they will run the city (or other governmental entity) like a private business and then they find out that governments are not like private businesses or corporations. Although some aspects may be run in a businesslike manner, such as wise purchasing policies, careful money management, and efficient management of staff, the overall management of a city or any other governmental entity can't be done like a business.

First of all, if you own a business, you make all the decisions based on what you want to do with your money and what direction you want to take for future development. You may seek advice from others but the final decision is yours to make and you will enjoy or suffer the consequences. Unlike private corporations or small businesses, governmental entities are owned by the citizens and funded by their tax dollars. Citizens elect people to make decisions about their quality of life in the city, school district, county, state, county, or country. It is an awesome responsibility because you can't base decisions on your personal wants, needs, and causes or on whether your decision might prevent your getting reelected. Decisions have to be

made on the basis of what is good for all of the citizens in the governmental entity in which you serve, not just today, but ten, fifteen, or
more years in the future. These decisions should not be based solely
on the demands made by the group of people taking turns at the
podium on any given day who are telling their representatives what
they want them to do and how they want them to vote.

Second, the thing which frustrated me most was that the wheels
of government turn very slowly. Some things take years to accomplish.
For example, if you see that a bridge in your city needs to be adapted
so that flood waters will not back up behind it, and that bridge is on a
state highway, you have to get it approved by one or more committees
and placed on the state schedule. If you can convince the state that
the project is valid, it may be planned for five years from the time you
make your request. Funding priorities are set on schedules that
include funding availabilities and so you have to wait. The bridge
project may occur long after you have left office and some other official may get the credit for the resulting benefits, but then you have to
know in your own heart that you did a right thing and be satisfied
with that, even if a small corner of your brain still hopes that
someday, somebody, sometime, will remember that you did something
good.

<u>Chapter 11:</u>

Quotes from City and County Officials and School Board Trustees, and 10 Basic Rules for Officeholders

You've heard of the expression "a word to the wise . . ." Here are words of advice to anyone considering a run for office, or who has just been elected to office, from some "wise" public officeholders from Texas who responded to my survey. Their wisdom comes from their personal experiences.

It should be noted that many of the officials have been elected or appointed by their peers to hold regional, state, and national offices in organizations composed of elected officials so they not only go the extra mile for their communities but take on the greater responsibilities of such offices. All have many years of experience in various volunteer organizations other than the offices which they held at the time of the survey.

I promised each public official who responded to my survey that, as one who has been misquoted more times than I ever dreamed could or would happen, I would present their quotes exactly as they were written as a thank-you gesture for their time and trouble in filling out and returning the survey forms. Here are quotes given to me by the public officials (all from Texas) who responded to my survey:

> Never run for public office or accept a public appointment to deal with the public unless you are able "to disagree without being disagreeable." Remember that "common sense makes the difference." *Kenneth Alley, Mayor Emeritus and City Founder, City of Leon Valley.*

> (Mayor Alley's quote is listed first because he was my primary mentor. After he retired from holding office and serving on various city boards, he continued to attend Leon Valley city council meetings and never failed to let the council know when it was doing a good job or when it was not performing up to par. An inspiration to all who believe in servant leadership and a true "Father of the City of Leon Valley," even in his nineties he still had that special fire within — when it came to city issues he expressed his opinions vigorously, but always following his own advice "to disagree without being disagreeable." As noted elsewhere in this book, our city mourned the passing of Mr. Alley who died in May 2006. He was an inspiration to so many of us.)

It (holding office) is the highest calling in a free society. *Tommy Adkisson, County Commissioner, Bexar County, and former Texas State Representative.*

Serving on the Leon Valley City Council was one of the most rewarding things I have done. I saw it as a great honor to have been elected so that I was able to be of service to the city and the citizens. Even today, 20 plus years later, I look back on the four years I served with a feeling of great accomplishment and pride. I have always felt that it was because I lived in a small community where everyone had the opportunity of taking part in community activities if they so chose that this great chance to serve on the council came to me. In a city the size of San Antonio (especially 20 years ago), I feel I would never have had this opportunity. I feel really fortunate that I could serve on our city's Council.
Charlotte Asch, former Councilmember, City of Leon Valley.

Public service is often rewarding; sometimes frustrating; usually fun . . . But it's always a statement that you care about your community and what happens in it.
James Barden, Judge, Medina County; former Mayor, City of Hondo.

Do all you can, while you can, and enjoy knowing that at the very least, you tried your best to make a positive difference in your community.
Hugh L. Bradley, Mayor, City of Levelland.

Simply stated, it was a pleasure and a privilege. My efforts were appreciated by those I represented and the community was always

supportive of our plans and actions. I didn't always make everyone happy but they respected that I was trying to do the very best for the most.
Barbara B. Christian, former Mayor, City of Terrell Hills.

✜ ✜ ✜ ✜ ✜

Make sure you have a passion for an issue(s) that will make a positive difference. If you don't, you may need to examine your reason for running.
Bonnie Conner, former Councilmember, City of San Antonio.

✜ ✜ ✜ ✜ ✜

Holding political office is a privilege which offers opportunity and responsibility for anyone. It's really an awesome responsibility to set taxes on a community and caution must be done when doing so.
Gerald Dubinski, Mayor, City of Olmos Park.

✜ ✜ ✜ ✜ ✜

It's not a good day unless I: (1.) Learn at least one thing; (2) Screw up at least two things.
Peter Fleischhacker, Mayor, City of Shavano Park.

✜ ✜ ✜ ✜ ✜

It is a very rewarding experience because you feel you are actually serving your people – your community – your country. On the other hand, it can be a two-edged sword. You're put under a microscope and put in a position where you can be second guessed and open to criticism. Everybody outside of politics and opposite to your board feels they're smarter than you; they can do a better job than you, and, have simple solutions to all the community's problems.

J. J. Gonzalez, City Commissioner, City of Harlingen.

Holding elective office is a wonderful opportunity to serve one's community. It has a unique set of benefits and challenges. It requires an ability to balance, develop consensus, and lead. I serve to ensure all voices are heard and considered, and to ensure that special interests, from whatever source, are the dominant voice but are tempered by the common good.

Art Hall, Councilmember, District 8, City of San Antonio.

The longer I'm here the more definite the line is between my supporters and enemies. You never stop campaigning because you have losses everyday by people moving, dying, etc. . . . Burn-out comes when the CAVE people win over the number of comments you get from supporters. Folks expect you to get elected and then you're on your own to make things happen. Sometimes it is so lonely, I want to go back and be unknown again.

As my final term is in its last year, I made a resolution to be true to myself first. Oprah Winfrey said (and I'm now following her advice) "Surround yourself with those that make you the happiest." I've done some 'weeding out' and now can be more productive and sleep well at night.

I'm NOT term limited, but I'm self-limited as to the amount of time, energy and money I will give away and take away from my family.

My worry is this thing called "public service" gets in your blood and I won't be happy and healthy without it. Perhaps I will continue in another venue.
Becky L. Haskin, City Council, District 4, City of Fort Worth.

✣ ✣ ✣ ✣ ✣

Holding an elective office is not always enjoyable but it is often satisfying. It is personally fulfilling to engage with others in shaping the life of a community.
Patrick Heath, Mayor, City of Boerne.

✣ ✣ ✣ ✣ ✣

It is the greatest experience in the world. Small town America is where the rubber meets the road. I want to look back and hope that in some small way, I made a difference in the town I grew up in and have called home for 53 of my 60 years. Some are made to watch as spectators, some are made to play the game. I thank God and the good people of Edna for letting me on the field of play. It has made my life better. I only hope I have helped others along the way.
Joe D. Hermes, Mayor, City of Edna.

✣ ✣ ✣ ✣ ✣

Every city council meeting is opened with the Pledge of Allegiance to the Flag. And every time I repeat the words "with liberty and justice for all" my thoughts turn to the fact that if we, as public servants, do not protect the "liberty and justice for ALL" who will?
Gloria H. Kehl, City Councilmember, City of Alamo Heights.

This is your city and you can help make it better. [What she would tell a newly elected city official.]
Ann Mabry, Mayor, City of Grey Forest.

I feel that we all have an obligation to serve others and make some contribution toward making our community and state a better place to live. There is no greater opportunity than to assume a leadership position in elective office. The rewards and feelings of accomplishment are indescribable!
Dr. Jerry Marshall, Mayor, City of Rotan.

When your trash isn't picked up, you don't call the governor. When the potholes aren't fixed, you don't call the lieutenant governor . . . You call my listed telephone number in the Corpus Christi phone book at 3 o'clock in the morning and tell me how bad I am.
Loyd Neal, Jr., Mayor, City of Corpus Christi, quoted in the San Antonio Express News, *3-28-2004, about Texas Governor Rick Perry's local property tax cap plan.*

Holding elective office in a small city can be as rewarding as it can be frustrating. Never forget that every decision should be for the best interest of the city as a whole and never expect the pat on the back — if that's the reason you ran for office then you will be very disappointed.
Jim Parma, Mayor, City of Selma.

❖ ❖ ❖ ❖ ❖

I will always be grateful that I had the opportunity to serve on City Council, although the time was all too short. I was just beginning to feel I had a good grasp of the workings of the council and could contribute more.

Volunteering has been a way of life for me, particularly since retirement. I wanted and needed to serve a larger purpose in life. Family demands no longer occupied so much of my time and the idea of serving in a larger capacity by being on the council appealed to me.

I have always enjoyed working with intelligent, up-beat, unselfish, forward-thinking people and I found them on the council. In addition, I have learned much about my city, its people and the workings of city government and have developed a great respect for those involved in this service.
Carol Poss, City Councilmember, City of Leon Valley.

❖ ❖ ❖ ❖ ❖

Holding office requires more time than you expect. It also requires the ability to listen, to talk reasonably, to accept criticism without being depressed by it, to study issues not only by reading but also by asking questions in depth, to act honestly and ethically at all times, and to stay focused on the real (not imagined) needs of the people you serve. You must expect to always be on display, because you're a public person whether you want to be or not.
Molly Pruitt, Board of Trustees, North East Independent School District, San Antonio.

❖ ❖ ❖ ❖ ❖

Elective office is NOT for everyone. However, we are currently short on GOOD legislators, city council and school board members. If "good" people, running for the right reasons are not recruited or encouraged to run — then we have some of the ineffective entities that we don't need. Run for the right reasons and make a contribution to your community!

Katie Reed, Board of Trustees, Northside Independent School District, San Antonio.

Stay true to your promises and do not be swayed by loud special interest groups.

W.D. Scott, City Councilmember, City of Hollywood Park.

When in office, do not have an axe to grind nor an agenda that will not benefit the majority of the citizenry; be open-minded; carefully study needs of the city; be available; be willing to serve, and spend the time that is necessary to accomplish the responsibility that you have been charged with.

Joe Singer, Mayor ProTem, City of Iowa Park.

Don't do it if your heart is not in it; don't do it for the money, because it's not there; don't do it if you think you will become a hero (of sorts), because you won't; don't do it if you have a big mouth, because sooner or later it will get you into trouble; don't do it for altruistic reasons, because the frustrations will do you in before your altruistic goals are accomplished.

But, if you believe that government is really the vehicle to accomplish certain beneficial things for the public, AND if you truly can bring something that's missing into the equation, and can stick it out for the long haul, then go for it!
William H. "Bill" Williams, Commissioner, Kerr County.

✛ ✛ ✛ ✛ ✛

It has been a wonderful experience. I have met and worked with a lot of good people. Not everyone can have their way, but I feel all citizens think their council works for them. Public service is very rewarding. It allows you the chance to help people. And, you receive the reward of giving service in return.
Henry Wilson, Councilmember, City of Hurst.

✛ ✛ ✛ ✛ ✛

I would encourage anyone that has a desire to serve, to run for local office. It gives you a feeling of satisfaction, to look back and see the changes you helped create.
Glenn Wortham, Commissioner, City of Sweetwater.

Ten Basic Rules for Public Service

Here are some of the basic rules for public service (and also in life) that I have collected from experience (mine and that of others), and from various seminars on how to run and serve in public life:

1. Always tell the truth; then you don't have to remember what you've said. Telling the truth includes saying, "I don't know" or "I'm not sure." Better to give no answer than the wrong one which will surely get published somewhere.

2. If people see that you are sincerely trying to do the right thing, they will forgive your mistakes. But don't try to fake sincerity; people are smart and they will eventually spot a phony. And when you are criticized, don't take it personally even when it sounds personal. You are the public figure so you will be the target of people who may be in a bad mood, who may have a chip on the shoulder, and so forth. If you treat even such people with courtesy, others will notice and you will win in the end.

3. Never assume anything. Especially don't assume everyone knows why you are proposing a plan or project. Don't assume that all people read newsletters, newspapers, watch news on TV, or get information any other way just because you do. Don't assume that all people think like you do and will agree with you because your cause (or project) is right, according to you. For example, I have met some people who really don't like chocolate; I can't imagine why, but they don't and never will!

4. Respect everyone for two reasons: First, because it's the right thing to do. Second, because the people that you stomp on as you climb up the ladder to success are the same people you will meet on the way down; and they will be mad as hell at you, and make your fall even worse than it is. The Golden Rule is: "Do unto others as you would have them do unto you." It's not just "Do unto others."

5. Remember the popular saying that minds are like parachutes — they function only when open. While the past is the foundation on which we build the present and future, and while the past should be remembered, we have to accept that the times, people, and situations change. An idea that didn't work five, or even one year ago may be just the best idea for current action and plans. Also, keep your ego in your pocket. Believe it or not, other people could know more than you do and could have better ideas than you have. It helps to think in terms of "we" and "us" instead of "me" and "mine."

6. Common sense is a valuable trait and mode in which to operate. Too many laws have been passed because too many

people were too unknowledgeable, too unethical, or just plain too unwilling to do the common sense right thing.

7. It's possible to disagree without becoming disagreeable. This goes back to respect for others' opinions, however erroneous they appear to you. Nobody wins when you compromise, but nobody totally loses either.

8. Flexible does not necessarily mean weak. Consider this old Japanese story about the Wise Bamboo: In the days of old Edo (Japan), a tall and proud pine tree and a flexible bamboo stalk grew on the side of a windy mountain. One day, both were threatened by the fierce winds of a typhoon (certainly a metaphor for political life). The pine tree stood tall against the wind while the bamboo bent to the ground, yielding to the force. The pine tree chided the bamboo, "Why do you not stand firm and strong against the wind like me? Why do you bend and sway? Have you no pride?" Throughout the night the typhoon became stronger as it tore across the mountain side. In the morning, when the typhoon had passed and the sun came out, the bamboo stood straight again, undamaged due to its flexibility in the wind. And the pine tree lay uprooted, torn from the ground by the winds and its stubborn refusal to bend. "Nuff said," as they say here in Texas.

9. When you need advice on legal matters while you are in public office, you have access to the attorney(s) who are contracted to serve your governmental entity and the city, county, or school board administrative staff. Save yourself and your government entity a lawsuit; take their advice on legal and other matters!

10. Finally, like that old Kenny Rogers song, know when to hold and know when to fold. When holding office becomes dreary; when you can no longer embrace new ideas; when you feel aggravated most of the time; when you can't make time to do the job properly; when you find yourself thinking that you know it all and have done it all, and when your heart just isn't in it anymore, it's time to quit and let someone else have a turn.

Chapter 12:

When It's Time to Go

I think that it's time to leave any job when it's not fun anymore, that is to say, when your heart is no longer in it. One of the signs is that your mind begins to close. For example:

- When someone comes up with a new idea and your first thought is "Why *won't* or *can't* this idea work" instead of "How can we make this work."
- Also, it is definitely time to go when your response to a new idea is "We tried that and it didn't work." But you are not remembering that you may have tried it five years ago and now different people are going to try the same concept with different methods in a different time.
- It's time to go when you have forgotten how annoying the GOBS and CAVE people were when you had new ideas, and a newcomer to your political scene tells folks that you are one of the GOBS or one of the CAVE people.
- When the job is no longer the highlight of your life, and when circumstances are such that you cannot be effective no matter how hard you try, it is time to go.
- If you can't see your actions and reactions to issues and ideas clearly, it helps if you have a spouse or good friends to let you know when your time is up — before the public tells you it's time to go!

When I decided it was my time to go, I was very ambivalent about my decision but I believed that with the current political climate in my city, it would be better for me and for the city if I did not seek reelection, even if many people urged me to run. I announced my decision and expressed my feelings about holding office with a speech given at city council and which some of the newspapers printed in its entirety. It is my quote for the final chapter of this book. Here is my speech:

It is customary, when the mayoral year election is called, for the sitting mayor to announce if she or he will seek reelection to office.

As many of you know, I have been deliberating about my candidacy for many months. I have been urged to run by my husband, by city staff, by our wonderful volunteers, and others in the city.

I love this job. I think government is the most exciting and fascinating experience I've had other than raising five children and trying to stay married for these past 50 years.

I love government but hate politics. Last May's council election was a throwback to the days when Leon Valley election campaigns were acrimonious, filled with half truths, downright lies, and personal attacks. Our EDC election was a repeat of the council election.

Such tactics polarize the public. And in my opinion, they make our city look bad. But the worst effect is that mean-spirited campaigns discourage good, competent, dedicated people from running for office — good people who would run for office to enhance the quality of life and reputation of the city instead of merely enhancing their own egos and promoting their personal issues.

Also, as many of you know, because I have been so ambivalent about seeking a fourth term as mayor, I have been marking my calendar with a "yes, I will run" on good days in office or "no, I won't" on the not-so-good days, with the idea of using the total yesses or nos to make the decision.

I should say also that some people have suggested that, if I choose not to run for mayor, that I run for a council seat so that I could have a vote, which is an interesting idea.

It is often said that politics makes strange bedfellows. I stopped writing on my calendar and made my decision after I attended a wake where a eulogy, which, in my opinion, should be a sacred thing, was turned into a political speech. And, my decision was confirmed when I learned that a couple of the political bedfellows had made a "deathbed promise to get Marcy Meffert out of office." When people hear this, first they laugh, and then they say that such a thing is more pathetic and sad than it is funny.

Could I deal with an ugly campaign such as we had last year? Certainly. You know the old Texas saying that it's not how long you've been around but the roads over which you've been dragged. I have been dragged and I can take it.

Could I run a mud-slinging campaign to win — to try to get those pivotal 200 votes? Sure. I reported news about this city years ago, and I have held office long enough to know "where the bodies are buried" and I have some mud to sling if I wanted to get down to that level.

But that's not my style. I have always chosen the high road. I have always run for the office and not against any person. When I had a vote on council, I tried to see both sides of the issue and select the one that was best for the city as a whole and for the city's future, not what was best for my reelection or suited my personal opinions. Because I respect councilmembers' rights to their opinions, as mayor I have never called councilmembers before a meeting to suggest how they might vote. Only once did I send a note to councilmembers to tell them that I believed that their vote was extremely detrimental to our city's future. I felt that it was my duty as mayor to do so.

I am proud of my years in office, years in which new progressive ideas became realities with the help of our extremely professional city staff, our dedicated volunteers, and the people who stop me at the supermarket, or at city events, or send me notes, to tell me that I've done a good job. When you try to do your best and people notice it, the positive feedback is really overwhelming, especially when you get support from people you didn't even know were on your side.

But, there is an old Kenny Rogers song that says "you gotta know when to hold and know when to fold. . . ." I want to fold while I can still hold — in my heart — the loyalty and encouragement I've received from city staff, the help I've had from past councils to take our city into the 21st century with progressive new ideas, and the support, volunteerism, and personal inspiration from our people.

Although I truly have loved this job, I shall not seek reelection for the office of mayor in 2004. I have had four good years as a councilmember and five wonderful, heartwarming years as mayor. But my heart isn't in it anymore.

I think an ugly mayoral race is bad for a small city for the reasons I've stated. I hope that we will have a cleaner race if I'm not in it. Also, it's time for me to have a personal life again. . . . I haven't had one for the past 6 years! I'm not sure I'll know how to act if I don't have meetings to attend!

To our very professional and loyal city staff, to those councilmembers who helped me lead the city, and to everyone who has supported me these past 10 years, especially my husband and family, I'd like to offer this chorus from a Josh Groban song*:

Your raise me up, so I can stand on mountains
You raise me up, to walk on stormy seas
I am strong, when I am on your shoulders
You raise me up . . . to more than I can be.

I thank you all.
Marcy Meffert, Mayor, City of Leon Valley, 1998-2004

---

* From album titled "Josh Groban" byBrendan Graham/Rolf Loyland, 2002, Universal Music Publishing Company.

I experienced and felt almost all of the joys and not-so-joyful things that my colleagues expressed in their quotes and would give the same advice that they gave to anyone contemplating a run for office or anyone who is in office. Their statements reminded me of the many controversial and other issues that were and were not resolved and, best of all, the good things that occurred during my four years as a councilmember and six years as mayor of the city I so deeply believe has tremendous potential.

As I prepared to write this book, I sorted out ten years' worth of newspaper clips, photos, notes, agendas, and other materials that I had saved; I read over the columns for weekly newspapers that I wrote as public relations/good news about our city, read newspaper clips about council meetings and the few times that I was able to vote as mayor. As I read, I realized that every minute I spent in office was worth every effort. In addition to the newspaper clips, what began to touch my soul was the stack of heartwarming, complimentary notes and cards that I received from the city staff, volunteers, and people in our city who became my friends as well as colleagues. I began to realize that while politics is about issues and policies, duties, and responsibilities, actually public service was about people. And I had met some truly wonderful, kind, loyal, and sometimes heroic people described elsewhere in this book. To be sure, many of the most dedicated public servants do not hold office but support those of us who do, and often without any recognition at all these dedicated volunteers contribute on a one-on-one basis to other people in the community. It was, as my colleagues have said, an honor and a privilege to serve with and for such people.

Again, doing good for goodness' sake, causing good things to happen for good people, and shaping the future of your community is a thrill like no other and well worth any sacrifice of time and energy. Holding public office is an opportunity to make a difference even if it is in only a small corner of this world, and I heartily recommend it.

So don't just sit there on your good idea . . . run for city council, school board, or any office in any organization, or volunteer to help someone else with a good idea.

And if you won't or can't run for office or volunteer to help someone else do it, please just go to your polling places and **VOTE!**

Editorial from The Echo, weekly publication of Texas Heritage Newspapers LLC, in Helotes, Texas, May 19, 2004, written by Editor Pat McIlhenny.

Meffert leaves legacy

Leon Valley Mayor Marcy Meffert is leaving office this month after serving two terms as a council member and three terms as mayor. During that time, she has proved to be a public official any city – of any size – would be fortunate to have.

Meffert presided with an even hand, listening to all sides of an issue, but being firm enough not to get sidetracked on unrelated matters. She followed the philosophy of Leon Valley Mayor Emeritus Ken Alley: that people can disagree without being disagreeable.

Meffert recognized that Leon Valley can not exist in a vacuum. She was active in such organizations as Bexar County Council of Mayors, Alamo Area Council of Governments and Texas Municipal League, where she worked with other elected officials on a variety of issues that benefited the community. Among other things, she laid the groundwork for small cities having the option of adopting an economic development sales tax and was instrumental in getting a grant for residential pickup of hazardous household waste. Meffert initiated Los Leones Student Art Festival, a unique art show for elementary through high school students sponsored by the City of Leon Valley, Northside Independent School District and Northside Education Foundation. She promoted other programs that gained recognition for the city.

Perhaps most important, Meffert encouraged others to serve on city commissions, boards and committees. She wanted others to discover what she did – that government is exciting and public service is a rewarding way to give back to the community. Leon Valley's Leadership Program, which introduces citizens to all phases of city government, is an extension of Meffert's belief that people working together can have a positive effect on their community. Though people leaving office are generally the ones who receive plaques and certificates of appreciation, Meffert gave a gift to Leon Valley residents: a plaque on a wall outside city hall. On it is inscribed this quote by anthropologist Margaret Mead: "Never doubt that a small group of thoughtful, committed citizens can change the world. Indeed, it's the only thing that ever has."

Marcy Meffert's enthusiasm, energy and insight will be misssed. She sought office to serve her community to the best of her abilities and her abilities have raised the standard for those who follow.